PERSPECTIVES ON THE

A BICENTENNIAL CONTRIBUTION

Published for Southeast Missouri State University

MERICAN REVOLUTION

EDITED BY GEORGE G. SUGGS, JR.

Southern Illinois University Press
Carbondale and Edwardsville
Feffer & Simons, Inc.   London and Amsterdam

Library of Congress Cataloging in Publication Data
Main entry under title:
Perspectives on the America Revolution.
 Includes bibliographical references and index.
 1.   United States—History—Revolution, 1775-1783—
Addresses, essays, lectures.   I.   Suggs, George G.,
1929-
E208.P47   973.3   77-5737
ISBN 0-8093-0827-4

*To my parents
with love and appreciation*

CONTENTS

PREFACE

The approach of the Bicentennial of the American Revolution provoked grandiose schemes and frenetic activity designed to celebrate this singular event in the life of the nation. The celebration took many forms which served to remind Americans, at least for awhile, of their revolutionary origins. Symbolic dumpings of tea into rivers and bays, the colorful and often dramatic reenactments of Revolutionary battles, the raising of Bicentennial flags over communities and universities, the launching of civic enterprises such as the planting of memorial groves, the mass marketing of Revolutionary mementoes, and the issuing of commemorative stamps, medallions, and coins were but a few of the popular expressions and reminders of the nation's revolutionary past. Yet the celebration had other dimensions. Symposia, lectures, books, scholarly papers, and revamped university courses concerning the American Revolution proliferated, focusing attention upon the origins, the ideals, the principles, and the impact of the Revolutionary era upon modern American life, and giving the Bicentennial exultation a more substantive and enduring quality.

This book originated out of the desire of Southeast Missouri State University to contribute something of permanence to mark the nation's two hundredth anniversary. Unwilling to wait until the Bicentennial year to begin the celebration, the University's Artist and Lecture Series Committee in 1972 incorporated into its annual programs through 1976 lectures on the American Revolution by distinguished historians of the Revolutionary era. Later, in the spring of 1975, a newly formed Bicentennial Committee concluded that a volume containing these lectures would be a significant and enduring contribution of the University to the Bicentennial celebration. Consequently, the publication of this book became a major project of the committee and received its full support.

Perceptive readers will immediately note that other than the Revolutionary era itself, there is no underlying theme connecting the work of the contributors to this volume. A word of explanation is therefore in order. At the inception of the lecture series, for various reasons the Artist and Lecture Series Committee gave no serious thought to the future publication of the lectures. Each contributor, therefore, was given nearly free rein in selecting his subject, the only requirement being that it be rooted in the Revolutionary era. For this reason, the essays in this volume have not been prepared around a central theme that would provide an essential unity. Furthermore, there was no attempt made to obtain any interpretative balance. This procedure—or lack of procedure—accounts for the disparate character of the essays.

The delay in the decision to publish the lectures created particular difficulties for several of the contributors which, in fairness to them, should be mentioned. Although all were asked to prepare lectures for a mixed or general audience with a high percentage of undergraduates, three—Don Higginbotham, James Morton Smith, and Carl Ubbelohde—were completely unaware that the University would eventually request permission to publish their lectures. When the request was made, they graciously consented to participate in the publication venture, despite the imposition of much additional effort to revise and modify their original essays.

Finally, in order to provide a somewhat rational structure to the volume for the convenience of the reader, the arrangement of the lectures has been changed from the order in which they were given. For example, although Don Higginbotham's "James Iredell and the Origins of American Federalism" (chapter 6) initiated the Bicentennial series, it appears last in the volume.

Without the substantial support and encouragement of a number of individuals, this volume would not have been possible. I owe a special debt to Dr. Charles R. Wiles, chairman of the Bicentennial Committee, whose unfailing optimism helped to resolve what appeared at times to be insurmountable problems in getting the idea of this publication accepted. To my colleagues Dr. Lawrence E. Breeze and Dr. Harold Dugger, chairman of the History Department, I am obligated for wise counsel and scheduling considerations, which have been invaluable. Both Dr. Mark F. Scully, emeritus president, and Dr. Robert E. Leestamper, president of the University, played a crucial role in arranging essential funding. Their awareness of the importance of this and similar projects to the academic life of Southeast Missouri State University has been gratifying. The staff of Kent Library of the University has provided enormous aid in locating and acquiring essential materials. Thanks are also due to the University's Faculty Grant Committee, which provided generous assistance in defraying the cost of manuscript preparation. Finally, on behalf of Southeast Missouri State University, I would like to thank each contributor to this book. Each accepted and interposed into his busy schedule additional responsibilities that went far beyond his obligations as a lecturer. Each knows the extensive debt that I and the University owe. We gratefully acknowledge that debt.

George G. Suggs, Jr.

Southeast Missouri State University
Cape Girardeau, Missouri
December 10, 1976

NOTES ON CONTRIBUTORS

Robert E. Brown has published *Middle Class Democracy and the Revolution in Massachusetts, 1691–1780* (1955), *Charles Beard and the Constitution: A Critical Analysis of "An Economic Interpretation of the Constitution"* (1956), *Reinterpretation of the Formation of the American Constitution* (1963), and *Carl Becker on History and the American Revolution* (1970). He is also coauthor of *Virginia, 1705–1786: Democracy or Aristocracy?* (1964). His articles and book reviews have appeared in many scholarly journals and over twenty anthologies have included portions of his work. He is the recipient of the Distinguished Faculty Award at Michigan State University, where he taught for nearly thirty years. He also held visiting appointments at major universities. Brown is presently Emeritus Professor of History at Michigan State University.

Jack P. Greene is Andrew W. Mellon Professor in the Humanities at The Johns Hopkins University and has recently completed a year as Harold Vyvian Harmsworth Professor of American History at Oxford University. He is the author of *The Quest for Power: The Lower Houses of Assembly in the Southern Royal Colonies, 1689–1776* (1963) and *The Reappraisal of the American Revolution in Recent Historical Literature* (1967). Greene has edited *Colonies to Nation, 1763–1789* (1967), *The Ambiguity of the American Revolution* (1968), *The Reinterpretation of the American Revolution* (1968), *Great Britain and the American Colonies 1606–1763* (1970), *The Nature of Colony Constitutions* (1970), and other works. He is also the joint editor of several volumes. He is a prolific contributor of articles and book reviews to scholarly journals and a recipient of major fellowships and research grants. Greene also has held teaching positions at major universities.

Don Higginbotham is the author of *Daniel Morgan: Revolutionary Rifleman* (1961) and *The War of American Independence: Military At-*

titudes, Policies, and Practice, 1763–1789 (1971). He is presently editing the writings of James Iredell of which the first two volumes have been published as *The Papers of James Iredell,* and he has underway a biography of George Washington. In addition, he is a frequent contributor of articles and book reviews to leading historical journals. Higginbotham has held visiting appointments to major universities, the most recent being the United States Military Academy. He is Professor of American History at the University of North Carolina at Chapel Hill.

James Morton Smith is Director of the Henry Francis du Pont Winterthur Museum. He is the author of *Freedom's Fetters: The Alien and Sedition Laws and American Civil Liberties* (1956), *George Washington: A Profile* (1969), and *Politics and Society in American History* (1973). He has edited *Seventeenth-Century America: Essays in Colonial History* (1959), *The Constitution: The Origins of American Federalism* (1971), and he has co-edited *Liberty and Justice: A Historical Record of American Constitutional Development* (1958). He has contributed numerous articles and reviews to major historical journals. In addition, he has been the recipient of many fellowships and research grants. His professional activities include service as a consultant and teaching appointments at major universities.

George G. Suggs, Jr., is Professor of History at Southeast Missouri State University. He is the author of *Colorado's War on Militant Unionism: James H. Peabody and the Western Federation of Miners* (1972). His many articles and book reviews pertaining to the labor history of the American West have appeared in various journals.

Carl Ubbelohde is the author of *The Vice-Admiralty Courts and the American Revolution* (1960), *The American Colonies and the British Empire* (1975), and *A Colorado History* (1965). In addition, he has coauthored *Clio's Servant: The State Historical Society of Wisconsin* (1972), and has edited and introduced *The Declaration of Independence* (1974). His numerous articles and book reviews have appeared in the leading historical journals. He has received Distinguished Teacher Awards from the University of Colorado (Boulder) and Case Western Reserve University. Moreover, he has had visiting appointments at a number of major universities. Presently, he is Henry Eldrige Bourne Professor of History at Case Western Reserve University.

PERSPECTIVES ON THE
AMERICAN REVOLUTION

INTRODUCTION

Two hundred years ago, more than a decade of agitation in Britain's North American colonies climaxed in the Declaration of Independence, a document which announced to the world the intent of the colonies to sever their imperial connection and to create an independent nation. The men of the Second Continental Congress who made the decision for independence have been described as "reluctant revolutionaries," reticent men who opted for a variety of motives to oppose the policies of Britain which increasingly threatened colonial interests and eroded the strong bonds of affection tying the colonies to the British Empire. By its very nature, dissent and resistance by whatever means to British authority for the purpose of changing imperial policy were a risky business. However, when the Founding Fathers consciously converted relatively peaceful resistance to outright rebellion not for the purpose of changing policy but rather to disrupt an empire in order to create a new nation, the enterprise of resistance assumed new dimensions of risk and importance which reflected both the extent of the dissatisfaction of the instigators of revolution and the depth of their commitment to a new order wherein their interests would be primary.

The events in the thirteen years from the ending of the French and Indian War (1763) to the Declaration of Independence (1776) partially explain the nature of colonial complaints and dissatisfaction with Britain. In trying to resolve the serious problems which the war had spawned, in attempting to cope with the altered relationship to the North American colonies that the war had produced, and in seeking to adjust to Britain's unchallenged preeminence as the leading eighteenth-century power, British officials made substantial changes in imperial policy which were interpreted in the colonies as a threat to the mutually profitable prewar relationship and to the individual liberties commonly associated with English citizenship. Responding to the recommendations of a succession of ministers beginning with George Grenville and ending with Lord North, Parliament enacted a series of laws which produced first a gradual but then an accelerated alienation, a loss of affection that could not be restored despite the repeal of certain of the laws, the modification of others, and the recognition of the tremendous consequences in that loss if permanent.

When coupled with executive orders, the spate of Parliamentary legislation passed between 1763 and 1776 worked as a powerful corrosive to the widely held assumptions and perceptions of North Americans concerning their individual status as Englishmen and the importance in the British Empire of their institutions, especially their assemblies. Although based on a long-held assumption of absolute authority, Parliament's assertion of its power to tax in the Sugar Act (1764), the Stamp Act (1765), the Declaratory Act (1766), and the Townshend Revenue Act (1767) did more than resuscitate a largely dormant and unused power in North America. In challenging the century-long practice of colonial assemblies to tax their own residents and generally to govern their own domestic affairs, these measures threatened the progressive and evolutionary development of nearly 150 years of colonial self-government. Significantly, although all these statutes were passed well before the infamous Intolerable (Coercive) Acts of 1774 (one of which struck a direct blow at self-government in Massachusetts by radically altering that colony's charter), they were enacted at a time when the suspension of assemblies by executive action was used more frequently to discipline and to impose obedience to Parliament's dictates.

Threats to the rights, privileges, and prerogatives traditionally associated with English citizenship also lurked in these statutes, especially in their enforcement provisions, and in various executive procedures. Legislation enacted between 1763 and 1776 upon the recommendation of Grenville, Townshend, North and others established and enlarged the vice-admiralty courts and their jurisdiction. Cases of alleged violations of the Sugar, Stamp, and Townshend revenue acts were now to be tried not in the regular county courts but in the vice-admiralty courts without benefit of trial by jury. The use of the writ of assistance (a general, blanket-type search warrant) was again authorized and placed in the hands of minor customs officials who proceeded to harass American merchants. Judges of the vice-admiralty courts were authorized to make rulings of probable cause which protected officials from civil suits by persons whom they had falsely charged with violating the revenue and navigation acts. Such protection raised the spectre of unlimited harassment of commerce by customs officers, as John Hancock, Henry Laurens, and others soon discovered. Moreover, the British navy was thrown into law enforcement when officials ordered units of the fleet to patrol the coast, the rivers, and bays of North America in order to prevent illicit trade with its attendant loss of revenue. When these procedures provoked widespread resistance—sometimes peaceful, sometimes violent—the British army (an estimated 7,500 regulars remained in North America following the French and Indian War) was thrown into the breach to preserve order.

Long before the battles of Lexington and Concord, perceptive Americans thought that they discerned a pattern of tyranny in Parliament's ready resort to extraordinary means, including military force, to impose upon them its limited definition of rights, its self-serving definition of sovereignty, and its restrictive, unitary concept of empire. Such readiness potentially endangered English liberties, some of which were thought to extend back in time to Magna Charta. The right to trial by a jury of one's peers when charged with a crime, the right to be free from unreasonable searches and seizures, the right not to have property taken without one's consent, the right not to be taxed without representation, the right to be secure in one's home—all seemed increasingly jeopardized by British ministers and a Parliament determined to have their way in North America whatever the cost. The result was a widening ripple of dissatisfaction, suspicion, and mistrust concerning the motives of Britain that embraced a growing number of Americans on the eve of hostilities. Many such Americans concluded that a deliberate conspiracy against liberty was underway, a conspiracy which had to be resisted.

In addition, many Americans concluded that the various statutes enacted after 1763 embodied a radically different economic policy from that of the prewar years, a changed policy that was potentially dangerous to the North American economy. Under the lenient administrations prior to the French and Indian War, various trade and manufacturing acts remained essentially unenforced, the Molasses Act (1733) being a prime example of this lax enforcement. Stimulated by such leniency, the colonial economy developed relatively free of inhibiting restrictions. However, postwar ministers, facing a new set of war-induced problems and circumstances, determined to reverse this unsystematic form of imperial administration. Their efforts generated additional anxiety and apprehension in America concerning the intent of the ministers and Parliament, because some of the measures noted above and others would clearly damage colonial economic interests. The Proclamation of 1763 hampered western land use and speculation; the Currency Act (1764) made colonial business transaction more difficult; the Sugar Act hampered trade with the French West Indies and struck a blow at the "triangular trade," so vital as a source of specie; the Quartering Act (1765) required the colonies at times to subsidize unwanted British troops stationed in America; the Sugar, Stamp, and Townshend revenue acts might accelerate the flow of specie from the colonies and accentuate the perennial problem of specie shortage. When considering the economic dimensions of the various acts passed between 1763 and 1776—even if the punitive Intolerable Acts were excluded, one of which disastrously closed the thriving port of Boston—some Americans concluded, perhaps erroneously, that Britain intended to relegate them forever to a position of economic subordination and inferiority within the empire. They therefore determined to resist.

For more than a decade after 1763, different British officials struggled unsuccessfully with imperial problems that were made increasingly complex by America's disobedience to law. Even so, they were not totally unresponsive to American opposition, especially when it created political and economic difficulties at home. For example, they grudgingly recommended to Parliament that it repeal the Stamp Act and that it also substantially modify the Sugar and Townshend revenue acts primarily because of America's strong adverse reaction to these laws. However, even when making these apparent concessions, they were careful never to concede officially an iota of power inherent in Parliament's claim of absolute sovereignty over the colonies. This claim was best expressed in the Declaratory Act which was passed simultaneously with the repeal of the Stamp Act. This adamant refusal to recognize any legitimacy in the American position concerning rights, the federal structure of the empire, and the divisibility of sovereignty became an important ingredient in American discontent. Parliament would not permit upstart colonists to redefine relationships within the empire—even if the new definition conformed to existing reality and fixed American loyalty to Britain; Americans would not permit Parliament to perpetuate the myth of its absoluteness—even if the price of their rejecting the myth was the destruction of the empire by revolution and war.

It was in this context that Parliament passed the Tea Act (1773) which provoked the Boston Tea Party, led to the enactment of the Intolerable Acts, and set the stage for a sharp confrontation between Americans determined to resist and British officials equally determined to rule. Force now became an essential factor both in the policy of resistance and the policy of enforcement. The predisposition to utilize force embellished the escalating moves and countermoves with new levels of commitment as each side analyzed and reassessed—all too frequently with misjudgment—the motives and actions of the other. Watching Americans prepare for resistance and fearing that their objective was independence, Britain resorted to means that reflected not affection for her American subjects but rather an antagonism of the type commonly reserved for enemy nations. Resistance leaders, believing that British officials were conspiring to destroy self-government, plunder their property, and reduce their liberties, increasingly resorted to means ordinarily foreign to loyal and obedient subjects. Thus lines hardened until war erupted in April 1775 at Lexington and Concord.

For the next fifteen months as civil war raged, Americans hesitantly groped toward a decision for independence. It was not until July 2, 1776, that they took the irrevocable step when the Continental Congress adopted a resolution of independence. Two days later, the Congress agreed to the Declaration of Independence. Thus the United States was launched. However, a War for Independence—a war that lasted for years and eventually involved France, Spain, and the Netherlands against Britain—was required to validate its existence as a free country recognizable as such by other nations. Out of their concerns and dissatisfaction with British post-1763 policy, Americans had gradually and reluctantly fashioned the start of a nation.

Succeeding generations of Americans have looked back upon their Revolution, pondered its significance, and searched for its meaning. Historians, particularly the professionals of the twentieth century, have subjected this epochal event to an unusually searching analysis, seeking to discover its causes and to find supportable conclusions concerning its consequences. The result has been a proliferation of studies which throw much light upon the Revolutionary era and the enormous complexity of the Revolution itself. However, no lasting interpretive consensus has emerged from these studies. As Robert E. Brown's "Did the American Revolution Really Happen?" (chapter 2) reveals, historians differ sharply on the causes, the nature, and the consequences of the Revolution. When Brown measured the work of Carl L. Becker, Charles Beard, Arthur M. Schlesinger, Sr., and other Progressive historians who advocated Becker's "dual revolution" thesis against the classic description of revolution found in Crane Brinton's *Anatomy of Revolution* (1938), he discovered that the historical evidence does not support their initial conclusion that the American Revolution was a successful class struggle to democratize American society which counterrevolutionists then overturned by maneuvering the adoption of the Federal Constitution. In his opinion, no such class revolution occurred in America. Instead, Brown concluded that there was indeed a revolution; however, it was a revolution that involved essentially a change of American attitudes toward the British—a change that began perhaps earlier than 1761 and ended in 1776—and that was intended to preserve America's existing democratic society from the assaults of British imperialism. In reaching this conclusion, Brown made important philosophical observations about the role of the scholar and his responsibility to the truth.

Although historians disagree concerning the causes, the nature, and the consequences of the American Revolution, they all naturally agree on one indisputable political result, the independence of the thirteen colonies from Great Britain and the creation of the United States. This incontrovertible result might suggest to some that from the beginning of their problems with Britain, the Founding Fathers had decided quickly upon independence and pursued it relentlessly toward the founding of a new nation. Of course, they neither acted so decisively nor so rashly. Carl Ubbelohde concluded in "The Idea of Independence" (chapter 3) that the decision for independence (even for rational men like Washington, John Adams, Jefferson, and others) was extremely difficult because although it took men down a road of expanded horizons, opportunities, and new vistas, the road was also crowded with uncertainties and dangers which involved lives, fortunes, and sacred honor. Consequently, it was not until the period 1774 to mid-1776 that most Revolutionary leaders confronted the idea of independence as an actionable concept, that is, independence as something to be worked for as an immediate, obtainable goal. Thereafter, it became a deliberate enterprise as resistance leaders, opting for independence, made positive judgments about such questions as the possibility of ultimate success, foreign aid from France and other powers, unity of the colonies in a common cause, economic survival as an independent nation, societal cohesiveness after independence, and a viable future. These and possibly other considerations, according to Ubbelohde, were the components of the idea of independence, most of which required an affirmative response by Revolutionary leaders. Time proved the correctness of their decision to embrace independence with its inherent risks rather than reconciliation with its less uncertain future.

In "The American Revolution: An Explanation" (chapter 4), Jack P. Greene examined the nature of the bonds between the colonies and Britain which made the decision for independence so agonizing for many Americans. For more than 150 years, habit, interest, and affection—not coercion—had effectively linked the colonies to Britain, a country which had served not only as the source of political, cultural, and moral authority but also as a source of pride and self-esteem. What finally weakened these ties and persuaded the colonists to sever their imperial connection? Greene found the answer in Britain's efforts to reinforce its political authority in North America after the end of King George's War in 1748, a reform effort that was interrupted by the French and Indian War (1754–63) but then intensified afterward in a much altered and more fragile context. Britain's attempts to reform the imperial system were misinterpreted by the colonists as abuses and grievances, from which sprang major misunderstandings such as the Stamp Act crisis. Greene concluded that revolution did not occur between the repeal of the Stamp Act in 1766 and the outbreak of hostilities in 1775 only because there existed powerful deterrents (for example, deep ties of loyalty and affection) which held the colonists to Britain despite their increasing dissatisfaction. It was not until significant developments occurred principally after 1773 (for example, the slow desacralization of the moral order binding the colonies to Britain) that the deterrents were sufficiently undermined to make revolution and independence more acceptable to influential Americans. The crisis produced by the Tea Act, the Boston Tea Party, the Intolerable Acts, and the resulting British-American moves and countermoves finally created the conditions necessary for revolution. Thus, in Greene's opinion, inasmuch as the Revolution might be said to have had a "sufficient cause," it was Britain's efforts to reform the imperial system and the colonists' perception of these efforts as a series of abuses which slowly and effectively destroyed the ties that had bound the North American colonies to Britain for over 150 years.

As British colonial relations deteriorated during the period 1763–76, moving gradually from a reasonably stable through a dysfunctional to a revolutionary situation in a process which Greene so effectively analyzed, Americans from all ranks of society became direct or indirect participants in the events that produced the Revolution. Resistance to Britain catapulted to the forefront an array of extremely gifted individuals who used their exceptional abilities first to seek reconciliation and then, when that had failed, independence. Among the extraordinary group was John Adams whom James Morton Smith in "John Adams and the Coming of the Revolution" (chapter 5) placed among the most brilliant men of the Revolutionary era. During the decade prior to 1776, Adams built a solid reputation as a practicing attorney in Braintree and Boston. Motivated by a burning desire for fame but yet constrained by a Puritan upbringing, a corrective self-criticism, and a high sense of duty, he early became involved in the resistance movement when he opposed the Stamp Act with publications which argued that it was an unconstitutional encroachment upon the inalienable rights of Englishmen in North America and which denied Parliament's claim to absolute power in the Declaratory Act. From 1765 to 1776, according to Smith, Adams was a conspicuous figure in the resistance movement around Boston where he used his legal and writing talents to the hilt in upholding American rights. Consequently, when Parliament provoked a new crisis by enacting the Intolerable Acts (1774), Adams was prepared for an even greater role as a delegate to the First and Second Continental Congresses. After reviewing Adams's work as a delegate, especially that performed in the Second Congress, Smith concluded that it was so important that had Adams died on July 3, 1776, his greatness would have been assured. Fortunately, however, his career prior to the Declaration of Independence was only the beginning of even greater service to the nation he helped to found. Adams later became a distinguished diplomat who helped to negotiate the treaty ending the War for Independence and who became the first American ambassador to Britain. He concluded his public career by succeeding Washington as president.

Adams ranked among the principal contributors to the Revolution and the early life of the nation. But the men who made the Revolution were not all Washingtons and Adamses. Some were secondary and lesser figures whose service, although not conspicuous, was nevertheless vital for the success of the Revolution and the survival of a fledgling nation. Such individuals provided a wide range of offstage service, frequently provided at great sacrifice, to the cause of independence. However, like the more important leaders, their initial resistance to Britain was to preserve American rights within the empire and not to gain total independence.

In "James Iredell and the Origins of American Federalism" (chapter 6), Don Higginbotham examined the work of a man who, although rising later to the rank of associate justice of the United States Supreme Court, is generally regarded as a secondary figure of the Revolutionary era. In essays between 1773 and 1776, James Iredell explored the problem of how to maintain the empire *and* guarantee the liberties of Americans. As a solution, he proposed a federal concept of empire, that is, to legalize the practical, working empire that had evolved over 150 years and whose structural and functional relationships largely satisfied most Americans. However, British officials rejected this solution because it placed constitutional limits to Parliament's power, and because it rested upon a concept of divided sovereignty. Their rejection made Parliament's idea of sovereignty and the colonial idea of rights totally incompatible. According to Higginbotham, this conflict forced Iredell and others such as James Otis to search for alternatives to an either-or choice between absolute sovereignty and total independence. Out of the search came the idea of an agency (for example, courts with the power of judicial review) to determine when Parliament exceeded its constitutional authority. However, by early 1776, Iredell realized that British officials would never accept any solution that reduced the power of Parliament, that in the conflict between power and liberty, they would not make concessions to liberty even to save the empire.

Higginbotham concluded that, although Iredell's intellectual efforts had failed to save the empire, his concepts of federalism which largely originated in the Revolution—sovereignty of the people, separation of powers, supremacy of fundamental (constitutional) law, judicial review—proved useful after 1776 in constructing a new nation.

The nation has moved into its third century. As historians continue to probe the many dimensions of the Revolution to gain new insights and perspectives into this singular event of our history, they will probably be no more successful than past and present-day historians in reaching a consensus concerning its causes, its meaning, its objectives, and its results. Nevertheless, the Revolution was a seminal experience from which flowed many of the values that undergird our national life. Like the essays which follow, future studies of the Revolution hopefully will be valuable in reminding Americans of their origins and the values which motivated the men who created this nation.

Robert E. Brown

2

DID THE AMERICAN
REVOLUTION REALLY HAPPEN?

In one guise or another, historians have been arguing for many years the question of whether the American Revolution really happened, but the general public, for the most part, has been unaware of this controversy. Most people probably assume that the celebration of the Bicentennial is proof enough that the Revolution really happened, especially since millions of dollars are being spent to commemorate it. So since this is the Bicentennial, perhaps the time has come for the public to be informed about the issues that have divided historians for so long.

Several questions are inherent in the problem. What do we mean by "revolution"? Are there conflicts with goals and accomplishments that are not "revolutionary," even though they are called revolutions? Are there different kinds of revolutions, and if so, do similar revolutions follow well-defined patterns of development? Is there such a thing as a law of revolution, and did the American Revolution verify such a law?

If, as appears inevitable, our problem hinges to some extent on the definition of "revolution," a good place to begin would be the dictionary. Random House defines revolution as 1) a complete and forcible overthrow of an established government or political system or 2) a radical and pervasive change in society and the social structure, especially when made suddenly and often accompanied by violence. Webster gives us about the same ideas—an overthrow of a government, form of government, or social system by those governed and usually by

13

forceful means, with another government or system taking its place. Webster goes further by equating the American, French, Chinese, and Russian Revolutions as analogous.

These definitions were not sufficient for a Harvard professor as a guide to an understanding of successful popular revolutions. In a book entitled *The Anatomy of Revolution,* Crane Brinton dissected four such revolutions—the English (1640), the American, the French, and the Russian—to show that striking similarities existed in their inception, development, and culmination. Brinton recognized that deviations among the four precluded the stating of a "law of revolution," but they all followed a pattern that approached something close to a law of revolution.[1]

Since historians have long used some of Brinton's ideas both before he wrote his book in 1938 and afterward, a detailed summary of Brinton's *Anatomy of Revolution* should provide a basis for an understanding of the American Revolution and its philosophical kinship with other of the world's popular revolutions.

As any good scholar should do, Brinton defined his terms in ways that most of us would doubtless accept. A successful popular revolution is one carried out in the name of freedom by a majority against a privileged minority. Tactics include violence, terror, purges, guillotines, and firing squads, and the result is the drastic and sudden substitution of one group for another in governing a territorial political entity.[2]

Brinton then developed six phases through which successful popular revolutions pass:

Phase 1. The society which produced revolution must be structured in a way that incites strong animosities among the lower classes. Usually this involves a corrupt, inept, privileged ruling class which dominates a discontented lower class deeply resentful of discrimination and ready to demand changes in the existing order.

Phase 2. Reformers and potential revolutionists are unable to achieve desired reforms in the existing political and social order, and thus become convinced that drastic measures are justified. Intellectuals, who are never satisfied with the status ctoral dissertation, *The History of Political Parties in the* New York, 1760–1776. Here he developed what known later as the Becker "Dual Revolution" thesis. rican Revolution was really two revolutions, he de- e of Americans against Britishers and one of lower- ricans against upper-class Americans. One was a f "home rule," the other of "who should rule at these two revolutions, however, Becker believed cond was fundamental, for it involved "the democ- of American society and politics."[8]

h Brinton's *Anatomy of Revolution* came later, Becker ollowed the pattern of Brinton's first and second is interpretation. For Becker colonial society was evil kind of class-structured society that would social revolution. It was a society of rich and poor, and underprivileged, enfranchised and disen- , conservatives and radicals, and throughout the n 1760 to 1776, radical, disfranchised lower classes ontroversy with Great Britain to muscle their way stocratic political arena. The buildup was such that expect Brinton's third stage, the point of armed be primarily a class war between upper and lower h the lower classes emerging triumphant.[9]

ton's third stage of the revolution never mate- ue, there were two antagonists, the "revolutionists" d regime, but unlike Becker's implied cleavage erican society, the revolutionists were Americans, ,000 miles from their antagonists, the British, and he minority party and not the majority. True, also, some Americans and Britishers in America who he British as loyalists, and some Englishmen who or favored the Americans, but their loyalties were on the basis of class interests. There was no mas- ntation of Americans against Americans as there hmen against Englishmen, Frenchmen against , and Russians against Russians in the other popu- ons described by Brinton.[10]

fourth phase not only did not occur, but what did ally refuted the entire Becker-Brinton thesis as far

quo, desert the old regime to strive for radical alterations of the prevailing system.

Phase 3. Failure of reform brings the emergence of two opposing parties, the old regime and the revolutionists. Since revolutions grow from seeds sown by men who desire drastic change, the time comes when constituted authority is challenged by illegal acts and armed conflicts result, with success going to the revolutionists.

Phase 4. Revolutionary momentum does not end with the initial victory of the revolutionists over the old regime, however, for victory reveals cleavages within the ranks of the revolutionists over how far they will carry revolutionary change. Moderates who would accept limited change are confronted by radicals or extremists who demand a complete regeneration of society based on their concept of what the good society should be.

Phase 5. Conflicts within the revolutionary party eventually culminate in The Terror, a period during which revolutionists not only execute members of the old regime, but each succeeding wave of radicals eliminates the more moderate members of the revolutionary party. Fanatical idealists seek to shape society in their own image, to create their own heaven on earth, and although they demand liberty and toleration when out of power, they now disdain liberties of others or forms of legality that block their goals. Authoritarian ideas lead to dictatorship, and the desire for a heaven on earth brings progressive hostility toward organized religion.

Phase 6. Eventually the excesses of radicals or extremists cause a conservative reaction, or Thermidor. Peace and stability become more desirable than bloodshed and fanatical social regeneration, with the result that radicals are displaced by conservatives who regain control of the revolutionary movement. Thus the revolution comes full circle, for having started from the right, it moves through moderation to various shades of radicalism or extremism, and then comes back to the right again with dictators such as Cromwell, Napoleon, or Stalin in command.[3]

In addition to definitions and a theoretical framework of

popular revolutions, a knowledge of the philosophical framework within which twentieth-century historians functioned is also essential to an understanding of the way they have interpreted the American Revolution.

There were two interlocking facets to the philosophy of history that prevailed among historians of the Revolution, one ideological, the other epistemological. On the idealogical front, the issue was whether the historian should be the detached scholar searching for objective truth or the committed historian using history to promote a desirable social philosophy. The epistemological issue concerned the questions of what constituted fact or truth, whether truth was absolute or relative, where the truth resided, inside or outside the mind, and finally, whether subjectivism would always preclude any attainment of objective truth even if the historian attempted to be the detached scholar.[4]

With these concepts of successful popular revolutions and of philosophy of history in mind, let us examine the interpretations of the American Revolution by twentieth-century historians to discover what they have contributed to our problem.

The historian who was most influential in both the ideological and the epistemological approaches to the American Revolution was Carl L. Becker. Becker had partaken of the philosophies of both Frederick Jackson Turner at the University of Wisconsin and James Harvey Robinson at Columbia University. Although Turner at one time deplored the falsification of history for political or social purposes, he was also anti-capitalistic in outlook and believed that each generation must rewrite history in the light of its own hopes and expectations. Robinson was also anti-capitalistic, believed for awhile in progress for the common man, and proposed that history should be used as the natural weapon of radicals against conservatives in the cause of social regeneration. These men laid the foundations for what came to be called the Progressive School of historians.[5]

Ideologically, Becker was the committed historian rather than the scholar. He, too, was anti-capitalistic in outlook and believed that the historian should employ history in the cause of the future good society which he saw as a collective democ-

racy. The business of history,
intelligent discontent and to fo
the idea of progress, the past w
much better, but the future wo
function of the historian, there
of the past so that men would
not backward to a golden age-
and exploit it in the interests

On the epistemological sic
relativism, subjectivism, and i
objectivism, and realism. He b
tion are difficult to distingui
facts, facts do not exist until t
and the historian's social phil
creates. Detachment, therefoi
and not only impossible, bu
mind is a dead mind that doe
work. It is more important
than to be detached or objecti
was fond of quoting Voltaire
history is only a pack of trick
that are justified if they se
finally, he declared that facts
with a little intelligent prom
son, whatever they are com

In short, Becker believe
regeneration of society, that
Since one could not be ob
always be a mixture of my
approach was to develop a l
history in the furthering c
should not merely reconstr
should turn on the past and
progress. Thus history beca
of the ideology of the hist
subjectivism and relativism

Having accepted the
"scholarship" should be use
ress, Becker incorporated k

ogy in a
Province
came to
The Am
clared, c
class Am
question
home."
that the
ratizatio

Althou
in effect
stages in
indeed t
produce
privilege
franchise
period fr
used the
into the a
one wou
conflict, t
classes, w

But Bi
rialized.
and the
within A
they were
they were
there wei
went with
fought wi
not decid
sive confr
was Engl
Frenchme
lar revolu

Brinton
happened

as the "American Revolution" was concerned. In April 1776, so-called conservatives in New York swept city and county elections, there were no contests in ten county elections, and as Becker admitted, the "unanimity" was due to the departure of the loyalists, not to a "radical" victory over conservatives. "Radicals and conservatives" became revolutionists and loyalists, and affairs "were directed by cautious and conservative politicans, who . . . were still determined to preserve the essential features of their ancient political system from what they conceived to be monarchical encroachments on the one hand, as well as from rash democratic experiments on the other."[11] Becker also admitted that the government under the New York constitution of 1777 was anything but radical, more evidence that the "Revolution" was not a popular social movement.[12]

On the epistemological side, Becker did indeed manipulate the facts to make them say what he wanted them to say. His thesis rested squarely on an undemocratic colonial society, a "fact" which he proved by use of two documents. One on the census of 1790 purportedly indicated that there were only 93 freemen-voters in the city at that date. The time, 1790, of course, was irrelevant to the Becker thesis which covered the years 1760–76, and, if true, which it was not, would certainly prove that the Revolution did not democratize politics. The other document, which he cited, but did not use, gives all the men admitted as freemen in the city from 1684 through 1790. This document was relevant, but unfortunately for Becker, it showed that there were hundreds of freemen, as many as 170 being admitted on a single day. In fact, an ordinance stated that anyone who engaged in a gainful occupation in the city had to be a freeman.[13] So New York City was already democratic, a fact which explains why there was no change in government except for the elimination of the British.

Unfortunately, however, historians did not read Becker critically either for his ideology or his epistemology. They seemed unaware of the fact that he had really refuted his own thesis of social revolution and that his thesis rested on one of the most flagrant violations of scholarly historical method on record. His general interpretation accorded well with Progressive ideology, and as a result, the Becker "Dual Revolution" thesis eventually became standard among Progressive historians.

The second major link in the Becker-Brinton class revolution and counterrevolution thesis was forged by Charles A. Beard in *An Economic Interpretation of the Constitution of the United States*. Unlike Becker, who stopped at 1776 and thus encompassed only the first three of Brinton's six stages, Beard concentrated on phase six, the Constitution as a Thermidor or counterrevolution. His book was published in 1913 at the height of Progressive demands for democratization of American society and politics through social legislation and amendments to the Constitution for direct election of senators and a graduated income tax. According to Beard, capitalists put over the Constitution in an undemocratic society by undemocratic conspiratorial methods in order to nullify the progressive accomplishments of the Revolution and thus protect their property. Implicit in Beard's book was the idea that if the Constitution was written by capitalists for their interests, Progressives could change the Constitution for other interests.[14]

Although they were largely ignored by other historians, there were major contradictions in Beard's book which refuted his thesis. He claimed that the Constitution was the product of capitalistic personal property, but his evidence indicated that about 95 percent of the country's wealth was real estate and that Federal Convention delegates held more real than personal property. Beard also contended that a mass of men were disfranchised, yet his own statements prove that most men could vote. And instead of a bitter fight over the Constitution, town voters in Boston, New York, Philadelphia, and other places gave the Constitution overwhelming support, three of the first four states to ratify were unanimous (they were all agricultural states), and the total vote showed 62.5 percent in favor, a landslide in American politics.[15]

In addition, there was an irreconcilable contradiction between the Becker and Beard theses that would continue in Progressive historiography. Becker implied, but did not prove, that the Revolution democratized American society and politics, while Beard claimed, but did not prove, that the Constitution was the product of an undemocratic society. If Becker's assumption of democratization was correct, the Constitution could not have been the product of an undemocratic society, as Beard claimed. On the other hand, if conservatives remained in control, as Becker's evidence seemed to imply, then there was no need for a conservative counterrevolution, for no social revolution occurred. But if American society was democratic both in 1776 and 1787, neither thesis would be valid, for there was no need for a social revolution or a conservative counter-revolution.

A third link in this unproved and contradictory thesis was added by Arthur M. Schlesinger, Sr. In a book, *The Colonial Merchants and the American Revolution,* Schlesinger followed Becker in depicting colonial society as undemocratic, but it was the upper-class merchants rather than a lower-class proletariat who initiated action. Merchants protested against British mercantile regulations after 1763, but had no intentions of extending to the lower classes the freedom that they demanded for themselves. The merchants started something that they could not control, however, for as the lower class took over, merchants had to choose between British imperialism and democratic lower-class domination. Some merchants became loyalists, some attempted to remain neutral, and some tried to guide the Revolution into conservative channels. Failing this, the merchants later participated in Beard's conservative counterrevolution by putting over the Constitution. In effect, Schlesinger linked the Becker and Beard theses without seeing the incompatibility of the marriage.[16]

Still no historian had dealt effectively with stages four and five of Brinton's *Anatomy of Revolution,* a gap that was presumably filled in 1926 by J. Franklin Jameson in a book with a suggestive title, *The American Revolution Considered as a Social Movement.* Unlike Becker, Jameson's Revolution began as a political movement but expanded into a social one, for once started, it could not be confined to narrow channels. The essence was a "levelling democracy," Jameson declared, and many aspects and institutions—status of persons, democracy, trade, slavery, manufacturing, land control, education, and religion—were all profoundly affected. The Revolution, therefore, was a real social revolution in the accepted sense outlined by Brinton.[17]

Again there were basic contradictions both within Jameson's work and between Jameson, Becker, and Beard. In seeking the essence of the Revolution in a "levelling democracy," Jameson declared that "the people" who adopted the Constitution in 1787 were much more democratic than the people who wrote the Declaration of Independence. If true, which it was not, this appears to support the democratization which Becker postulated but did not prove; but at the same time, it contradicts Beard's contention that the Constitution was the product of an undemocratic society. Actually, Jameson contradicts himself by saying that few men were disfranchised before 1776 and that democracy did not really come until 1840. The fact is that Jameson's entire "social revolution" can be explained logically on the proposition that the elimination of Great Britain as a factor in American affairs allowed Americans to do many things that previously they had not been permitted to do.[18]

Perhaps the most interesting aspect of Jameson's book is the fact that he anticipated to some extent the Brinton book on *The Anatomy of Revolution*. Jameson defined popular revolutions as those involving a transfer of power from the hands of a smaller to those of a larger number of people, or from one great section of the population to another. These new rulers would then shape society in accordance with their desires and interests. But revolutions have their own natural history, Jameson continued, and as they progress they fall into the hands of men with increasingly extreme views. Consequently, the men who finally determine the social consequences of revolutions are not necessarily those who initially instigate revolutions.[19]

In this parade of Revolutionary theorists, Jameson was followed by Brinton, but anyone who reads Brinton critically must realize that the American Revolution should not be viewed as analogous to the English, French, Russian, and other more recent social revolutions. Brinton often excluded the American Revolution from his discussion, or his exceptions relative to the American Revolution are so numerous as to make comparisons meaningless. In addition, Brinton assumed that he could depend upon the work of other historians who have dealt with the American Revolution, and thus he incorporated the Progressive thesis with all of its contradictions into his own work.[20]

Finally, in 1940, Merrill M. Jensen attempted to tie the entire thesis together, even to its unresolved contradictions. Like Becker and others, Jensen assumed an aristocratic colonial society filled with class antagonism between rich and poor, privileged and underprivileged, enfranchised and disfranchised, conservatives and radicals. The Revolution was a true Beckerian social movement to democratize American society and politics, he believed, for the Declaration of Independence embodied radical political and social philosophy, the Articles of Confederation which followed represented a radical victory over conservatives, and democracy functioned without fetters under democratic state constitutions. Quite naturally, the Constitution, according to Jensen, followed the Beard pattern of conservative counterrevolution.[21]

Like the other Progressives, Jensen also failed to resolve the contradictions. He appears to accept Becker's claim that colonial society was undemocratic and that the Revolution brought democracy, but Becker's *evidence* shows that democracy had already arrived before 1776 and Becker admitted that the New York constitution was conservative rather than radical. If the Declaration of Independence, the state constitutions, and the Articles of Confederation all represented democratic victories for radicals, then society was democratic in 1787 and Beard's counterrevolution was wrong. Furthermore, if there was so much gain for democracy, why would democratic state legislatures send conservative capitalists to write a conservative Constitution that would undermine their base of power?

Since most historians did not recognize these inconsistencies, there were only a few sour notes in the entire orchestration of this Becker, Beard, Schlesinger, Jameson, Brinton, Jensen thesis. Some reviewers of Beard's book on the Constitution accused Beard of being a Progressive polemicist, influenced by Karl Marx and writing to promote socialism. But initial reviews were countered by those favorable ones which declared that Beard had exposed the Founding Fathers as conservatives who placed the dollar above the man while Progressive reformers in 1913 were placing the man above the dollar. Then in 1934 an obscure historian named Theodore Clark Smith accused Beard of fostering Marxian economic determinism, of writing popular history with Becker and other Progressives to promote collective democracy, and of fostering a philosophy of historical relativism that dictators in Europe were using to undermine democratic governments. Smith's attack forced Beard and his publisher, Macmillan, to issue a new edition of *An Economic Interpretation* with an introduction denying Smith's charges. With the historical profession rather solidly committed to Beard, however, this tempest in a teapot was soon forgotten.[22]

Part of the confusion over the revolution-counterrevolution thesis began to disappear about the time that Brinton and Jensen were rounding out the contours of the thesis. Ironically, the dispellers were the original architects of that confusion—Carl Becker and Charles Beard. As T. C. Smith had warned in 1934, Hitler and Stalin were employing historical relativism in Europe to warp men's minds and to undermine democracy. The destruction of freedom and democracy brought both Becker and Beard to a new appreciation of the democracy that they had so long criticized.

The first to break was Carl Becker, who was appalled by what he saw in Europe. Becker came to realize that the same prostitution of scholarship to achieve the "good society" of collective democracy could also be used to achieve a "good society" that called for the extermination of six million Jews. It all depended on whom the pack of tricks was being played. Now the benefits of American democracy far outweighed the evils, and in particular, American society before the American Revolution took on a different glow. Far from being the kind of society that generated social revolution, as he once believed, Becker now declared that eighteenth-century Americans "enjoyed a greater degree of political liberty, social equality, and widely based material prosperity than has ever fallen to the lot of any other people."[23] In addition, the Declaration of Independence that he had previously described as full of glittering generalities became the great charter of human freedom filled with generalities that still glittered.

Becker also abandoned much of historical relativism along with his ideology. Once he had believed that history was only a pack of tricks that we play on the dead and that facts could be manipulated to say what we want them to say. Now he declared that in the long run, all values are inseparable from the love of truth and the disinterested search for it. The Carl Becker of 1945 was no longer the same man who had won the resounding applause of his fellow historians when he was president of the American Historical Association.[24]

Like Becker, Beard experienced a conversion as he, too, witnessed the threatening triumph of dictatorship. In two books, *A Basic History of the United States* and particularly in *The Republic,* he presented a much more favorable view of the Constitution and the American democracy in general than he had previously done. Instead of a reactionary or Thermidorean document, the Constitution now embodied values that Beard had somehow previously failed to recognize.[25]

Although Becker and Beard suggested during World War II that their interpretations of the Revolution as a class revolution and the Constitution as a conservative counterrevolution might have been something less than accurate history, neither lived to see the final outcome of their admission. Becker died in 1945 and Beard followed in 1948. Yet within a few years, both the Becker and Beard theses would be subjected to severe criticism, and neither, according to their critics, would meet the test of scholarly history. Out of the research that was published after 1950 emerged an interpretation almost diametrically opposed to the Becker, Beard, Schlesinger, Jameson, Brinton, Jensen thesis.

This later research seemed to justify Becker's World War II confession that American colonial society provided a greater degree of political liberty, social equality, and widely based material prosperity than had any other society. Instead of being class-ridden, as Progressives indicated, it was probably the most middle-class society that ever existed in a developed country. Cheap land and high wages enabled most men to acquire property, and property conferred political rights that led to democratic colonial governments. Since colonial society was not the kind that was conducive to class revolution, it appeared that the entire Progressive thesis rested on a foundation of quicksand.[26]

If colonial society did not fit the description assumed by Progressives and Brinton as an essential basis for a popular revolution, neither did the second phase fit the script. Instead of class conflict by a majority against a privileged minority for social gains, the period from 1763 to 1776, as shown by this later research, witnessed a contest between a middle-class democratic colonial society and British mercantilism and imperialism. For many years, the British had followed a policy that colonies should exist for the economic advantage of the Mother Country and should be regulated politically to assure that benefit. European wars and colonial domination of British-appointed officials through control of salaries and appropriations had rendered British colonial policy ineffective, while at the same time rapid colonial increase in population and wealth posed the possibility of eventual colonial independence. Consequently, British measures after 1760 were designed to impose British authority over the colonies and thus to head off the threat of colonial independence.[27]

Quite naturally the British could not restore their authority over the colonies without curtailing the democracy that existed, and it was this threat to democracy in all its phases that brought colonial opposition. The use of writs of assistance, customs officials, and admiralty courts to enforce mercantilism, and the taxing of the colonies in the Sugar, Stamp, Townshend, and Tea Acts to raise money for the payment of officials' salaries all met stubborn resistance. And the final resort to troops at Lexington and Concord resulted in bloodshed as Americans refused to relinquish long-enjoyed political, economic, and religious liberties.[28]

Like the first phase, then, the second phase of the Revolution was almost the complete antithesis of the Progressive-Brinton second phase. Instead of an oppressed majority attempting to wrest rights from a privileged minority, the

Americans were the minority compared with the British. The Americans were not dissatisfied with their colonial governments, they were not attempting to bring social change, but they were, in fact, determined to keep what they had. The impetus for change came from the British, not from lower-class Americans, and there can be little doubt that American democracy would have suffered severely if the British had been successful.

If we can say that the Declaration of Independence marked the third phase of Brinton's anatomy of revolution, we must also say that the Declaration signified a War for Independence rather than an American Revolution. Naturally the two opponents had reached a point where differences were to be settled by armed conflict, but the real issue was whether Britain or America would govern the Americans, not whether control would fall into the hands of the lower classes.

What happened after the Declaration, that is, during Brinton's fourth phase, also confirms the interpretation that Americans were attempting to preserve what they already had. Except for the elimination of British power, the state constitutions bore a remarkable resemblance to the colonial governments that preceded them. They were middle-class, stake-in-society governments with property requirements for voting and holding office, bills of rights to safeguard civil and religious liberty, and often checks and balances to prevent extremes in government. The elimination of the British factor was naturally important, but there is no evidence that "radicals" had emerged triumphant to regenerate society.[29]

Neither did the American Revolution witness the fifth phase of radical takeover from moderates and The Terror as more radical groups liquidated less radical groups. Leadership at local, state, and Confederation levels remained remarkably stable, for most of the outstanding Americans in the period 1774–76 were still prominent after 1776. The internal conflicts were the usual liberal-conservative differences over ends and means that had been present in American society before the Revolution and have continued down to the present time. Some loyalists or British sympathizers remained, but their treatment was remarkably lenient unless they gave outright aid to the enemy. But there was no terror as there was in the other three popular revolutions.[30]

The sixth and last phase of the Revolution, Beard's conservative counterrevolution in the form of the Constitution, came under particularly heavy fire after 1950. Two chief methods were used. One was a chapter by chapter scrutiny of Beard's historical method to examine his use of evidence and the validity of the generalizations that he drew from his evidence;[31] the other was to complete the research which Beard outlined as essential but did not do, and then to test his thesis in *An Economic Interpretation* on the basis of this evidence.[32]

Both methods brought similar devastating results for the validity of the Beard thesis. In fact, one could use Beard's evidence to prove a thesis almost diametrically opposed to his own. Most adult men could vote and Convention delegates were perfectly aware that the document which they constructed would have to meet popular approval. The state legislators who elected delegates and the delegates themselves represented a great variety of economic interests, but especially real estate rather than personal property. There was wide support for drastic revision of the Articles of Confederation. During ratification, the Constitution was exhaustively debated, there was much apathy among the voters, a majority of all groups favored ratification, and the Constitution received a 65 percent majority in the ratifying conventions—again, as I have said, a landslide victory in American politics.

So instead of The Terror which brought dictatorship and tyranny in the English, French, and Russian Revolutions, the sixth phase of the American Revolution—the Constitution—resulted in what has been called merely the completion of the Revolution under a central government that was essentially middle-class and republican. In addition to being adopted by a landslide, the Constitution would undoubtedly have received a much greater majority had it contained a bill of rights.

If the revisionism of the 1950s completed the demolition of Beard and Becker's theories that they themselves had started during World War II, it also resulted in the late conversion of Arthur M. Schlesinger, Sr., from Progressivism to revisionism.

Unlike Becker and Beard, Schlesinger had remained a Progressive until after 1960. In a 1960 foreword to the paperback edition of Becker's *History of Political Parties,* Schlesinger praised the book as "a minor classic in historical literature" and "still a seminal work for students of the American Revolution." "In research method as well as in content, objectivity and interpretation," he continued, "it is a model of what a work of historical scholarship should always strive to be." Yet within a few years, Schlesinger wrote a manuscript on American colonial society that annihilated both the Becker thesis and his own earlier interpretation. When this book appeared as *The Birth of the Republic* in 1968 after Schlesinger's death, he was severely criticized as an apostate who had sold out Progressive history.[33]

Revisionist research and the recantation by some of the chief architects of the social revolution-counterrevolution thesis should have settled the question of whether or not the American Revolution really happened, but such was not true. Like old soldiers, widely held and emotionally accepted interpretations die hard, and the Progressive interpretation has been no exception. Scholars who have a stake in the thesis, professors who received their training before the revisionism of the 1950s, and people in general who are sympathetic with the social aims of Becker and Beard still adhere to the Progressive thesis. Even the gross violations of accepted scholarly standards have been justified on the ground that these historians were promoting desirable ends. Marginalia on library copies of books written by critics of Becker and Beard indicate that the emotional attachment to the old order is still very strong among students or faculty.

Of particular significance in recent times has been the efforts of a post-revisionist school, the "New Left," to refurbish the class-struggle and social revolution interpretation of the Progressives or "Old Left." Operating within the milieu of the Vietnam War and the student uprisings, the New Left historians have attempted to revive the notion of an elitist or deferential colonial society and the Revolution as a great social movement, thus making the American Revolution a legitimate prototype for other social revolutions. To this end, they write history "from the bottom up," as they say, rather than from "the top down" to emphasize the role of the common man, and like the early Becker, Beard, and others, they stress conflict rather than consensus in history. Unfortunately for their interpretation, however, they have become divided among themselves over whether America's class war occurred at the time of the American Revolution or at the time of the Civil War.[34]

Critics of revisionism have erroneously assumed that if the revisionists are correct, the American Revolution must be viewed as a conservative movement. Nothing could be further from the truth. A war to preserve a liberal society must be a liberal or democratic war, and in that sense, the American Revolution was a liberal or democratic war. We should remember that French revolutionists approved of American society as a model for themselves, and French revolutionists were not exactly conservative.

Although the revisionists have shown that the war of 1776 was really a War of Independence rather than a revolution, perhaps we should examine briefly some of the views of the men who were there before we make a final decision. John Adams is a reasonable starting point, and while it is too late to impeach our second president if he did not tell the truth, he was there, he was intelligent and articulate, and he was sufficiently conservative to have recognized class conflict if it had existed.

Adams confirms the revisionist interpretation of the "Revolution" as a movement of preservation rather than change, but he also reveals other important aspects of that significant event:

But what do we mean by the American revolution? Do we mean the American War? The Revolution was effected before the war commenced. The Revolution was in the minds and hearts of the people; a change in their religious sentiments of their duties and obligations. While the king, and all in authority under him, were believed to govern in justice and mercy, according to the laws and constitution derived to them from the God of nature and transmitted to them by their ancestors, they thought themselves bound to pray for the king and queen and all the royal family, and all in authority under them, as ministers ordained of God for their good; but when they saw those powers renouncing all the principles of authority, and bent upon the destruction of all the securities of their lives, liberties, and properties, they thought it their duty to pray for the continental congress and all the thirteen State congresses, &c.

There might be, and there were others who thought less about religion and conscience, but had certain habitual sentiments of allegiance and loyalty derived from their education; but believing allegiance and protection to be reciprocal, when protection was withdrawn, they thought allegiance was dissolved.

Another alteration was common to all. The people of America had been educated in an habitual affection for England, as their mother country; and while they thought her a kind and tender parent, (erroneously enough, however, for she never was such a mother,) no affection could be more sincere. But when they found her a cruel beldam, willing like Lady Macbeth, to "dash their brains out," it is no wonder if their filial affections ceased, and were changed into indignation and horror.

This radical change in the principles, opinions, sentiments, and affections of the people, was the real American Revolution. [35]

There is not even a hint of "social revolution" in Adams's account. The real revolution was intellectual and emotional, it began long before the War for Independence, and it was directed against British imperialism as a threat to the security of lives, liberties, and properties that Americans already had. Obviously it involved a conflict between Britain and her American colonies, not local class warfare to gain rights that lower-class Americans desired.

On another occasion, Adams added some important details to his "imperial" interpretation of the "Revolution." "The revolution was in the minds and hearts of the people, and in the union of the colonies; both of which were substantially effected before hostilities commenced," he declared. It really began in February 1761, when James Otis argued against writs of assistance, and it involved the appointment of a committed judge as a tool of imperialism. When Judge Stephen Sewall, "an enlightened friend of liberty," died, Governor Francis Bernard appointed Thomas Hutchinson to fill the vacancy "for the very purpose of deciding the fate of the writs of assistance, and all other causes in which the claims of Great Britain might be directly or indirectly implicated." But Otis not only exposed the insidious designs of writs, he also

laid open the views and designs of Great Britain, in taxing us, of destroying our charters and assuming the powers of our government, legislative, executive, and judicial, external and internal, civil and ecclesiastical, temporal and spiritual. . . .

Here, then, Sir, began the revolution in the principles, views, opions, and feelings of the American people. Their eyes were opened to a clear sight of the danger that threatened them and their posterity, and the liberties of both in all future generations.[36]

So again Adams refuted the Progressive-Brinton view of the "Revolution." It was imperial, not class, and its purpose was to preserve the civil and religious liberties that Americans already enjoyed and that were endangered by British efforts to destroy colonial governments through writs and other measures. Adams also included the union of the colonies in opposition to imperialism as an important element. So Adams's "Revolution" began in 1761 and ended with the Declaration of Independence which signified colonial union in 1776. Having completed their union and their "Revolution" in thought and feeling against British imperialism, the Americans then fought a War for Independence.

While it is not germane to our problem, it is of some interest in a Bicentennial year to note that Adams would have celebrated the culmination of the Revolution at a different time and by somewhat different methods than we celebrate it. Writing to wife Abigail on July 3, 1776, Adams declared:

Yesterday the greatest question was decided which ever was debated in America, and a greater, perhaps, never was nor will be decided among men. A Resolution was passed without one dissenting Colony "that these United Colonies are, and of right ought to be, free and independent States. . . ." The second day of July, 1776, will be the most memorable epocha in the history of America. I am apt to believe that it will be celebrated by succeeding generations as the great anniversary festival. . . . It ought to be solemnized with pomp and parade, with shows, games, sports, guns, bells, bonfires, and illuminations, from one end of this continent to the other, from this time forward forevermore.[37]

Adams was prophetic. We do celebrate the Declaration of

Independence with pomp and parade, but until they became illegal, we did it mainly with Chinese firecrackers on July 4 rather than July 2.

Another Adams, Samuel, referred to the conflict as a revolution, but like John, he, too, believed that the Declaration of Independence marked the end rather than the beginning, and that it was an unusual revolution. The major problem was the union of thirteen disparate colonies in a common cause, he said, and because of different interests and views, the process necessarily had to be slow. But having achieved this union with the Declaration of Independence, Adams declared: "Was there ever a Revolution brot [*sic*] about, especially, so important as this without great internal Tumults & violent Convulsions!"[38]

Like John and Samuel Adams, Alexander Hamilton also employed the word "revolution" to describe what happened, but again his description was that of a revolution to preserve rather than to achieve. Writing in 1794, he contended that Americans were "a people who originally resorted to a Revolution in Goverrt as a refuge from encroachment on rights and privileges *antecedently* enjoyed."[39]

On the strength of these three witnesses, we can say that the American Revolution really did happen, but we would have to admit that it did not fit the dictionary definitions nor follow the pattern of revolutions that Crane Brinton laid out in his first three phases.

In later life, another contemporary, Thomas Jefferson, looked upon the British-American conflict as a "civil war" between two different peoples who were already separated in fact if not in form. He did not believe that the Declaration of Independence created a new situation, but merely made explicit what actually existed. Like the Scots before the union with England, he said, Americans had always been independent of the people and Parliament of Great Britain.[40] This is the commonwealth idea as expressed in the Albany Plan of Union in 1754 and the Galloway Plan of Union in 1774. The Declaration of Independence and the fighting broke the only link in the commonwealth, the king.

While the Declaration of Independence itself was directed at the king as the link in the disintegrating commonwealth, it also shows that the king was the instigator, the "revolutionist," not the Americans. As Jefferson wrote, the time had come "for one people to dissolve the political bands which have connected them with another" since "a long train of abuses and usurpations" demonstrated the king's design "to reduce them [the Americans] under absolute Despotism." Then followed twenty-seven charges against the king, all relating to the mercantile and imperial policies by which he had proved himself a tyrant, "unfit to be the ruler of a free people." Because of the circumstances of emigration and settlement, Parliament had no right "to extend an unwarrantable jurisdiction" over these free people. Thus the break came because the king, aided by the unwarranted cooperation of Parliament, was attempting to deprive Americans of freedom that they already enjoyed.

So to the original question, "Did the American Revolution really happen?" my answer is yes and no. Yes, if we mean that it involved a change in American attitude toward the British, that it began in 1761 (or earlier) and ended in 1776, and that it was a movement to preserve a democratic society from the encroachments of British imperialism. But no if we mean that it involved class warfare between lower and upper classes to democratize American society and politics, that it succeeded through the Declaration of Independence, the state constitutions, the Articles of Confederation, and social legislation, only to be thwarted in the end by the adoption of a counter-revolutionary Constitution. I would agree with the Frenchman Alexis de Tocqueville that America by the early nineteenth century had never experienced a class revolution because it had never needed one.[41]

In this Bicentennial year it seems to me that the history of the American Revolution has a message for scholars as well as for the people in general. Since fact and truth are one and the same, and since they encompass everything that is and everything that was, the subject matter of the historian is the absolute truth of the past. The function of the scholar is to discover this truth to the best of his ability, whether he deals with the present or the past, with humans or with things. The late conversion of Becker, Beard, and Schlesinger demonstrates what happens when scholars forget their functions. In terms of ethical standards for scholars and politicians, I see little difference between Watergate and the falsification by scholars of historical evidence as methods to achieve desired ends. Good causes do not need false prophets, for as Carl Becker said, in the long run all values are inseparable from the love of truth and the disinterested search for it.

3

Carl Ubbelohde

THE IDEA OF INDEPENDENCE

We mark occasions in peculiar ways. As individuals we think of certain "milestone" birthdays in our lives, and the same is true of nations and the peoples who inhabit them. In 1826 America celebrated its fiftieth year of independence. It must have been a tragic-sweet occasion for (as those of you who remember well your fourth-grade history will recall) Thomas Jefferson and John Adams both died on that day. The country then was young and moving into the time of enthusiasm and exuberance historians have called the Age of Jackson. And in 1876 the nation marked its centennial year in an era clouded by a president impeached, a presidential administration corrupted, an economy unhinged and depressed—a time, if you will, that was not the happiest of eras. In the nation's sesquicentennial year—1926—the people's mood again had changed. That was the time of the fabled Twenties, before Americans had known what want and war would bring before midcentury. And now, as we approach the bicentenary, we find ourselves experiencing what others earlier have known: how difficult it is to be members of a society of other human beings.

That also was true two hundred years ago when Americans began to face perplexing problems as they thought about their options: continued political connection with their parent state Great Britain—or independence. In fact, it was particularly true two hundred years ago. In February 1775, the American people who paid attention to such things (and one assumes that many of them did so) knew that the Continental Congress, meeting the previous autumn, had hurled a challenge across the Atlantic Ocean. The British government had been both requested and advised to begin redressing American grievances. If it failed to do so, the Congress would meet again in the spring of 1775.

We know also that during that winter—January and February and March—of 1775, congresses and committees in the separate provinces articulated grievances and principles and, in a less rhetorical, perhaps more practical way, began to organize militia and to collect arms and ammunition in order to face the worst—if the worst should come. Very obviously, two hundred years ago, the American people were fast approaching a time of decision.

Affairs between Great Britain and her colonies on this side of the Atlantic Ocean now had entered what was to be the final, critical stage. The next few months would bring events that would entail highly dramatic consequences. Within nine weeks New Englanders would meet red-coated British soldiers at Lexington and Concord and a shooting war would commence. Within a year and a half, at Philadelphia, the Continental Congress would debate openly—and finally pronounce in a memorable declaration—separation from the British Empire.

I believe that the Americans responsible for those events of two hundred years ago were reasonably rational human beings who knew what they wanted. They did not stumble blindly into acts committing their lives, and their fortunes, and their sacred honor. I believe it unlikely, given the dangers and risks their activities entailed, that they were unaware of, or unconcerned about, their objectives. They had some idea of the goals they hoped to attain.

If the assertions in the preceding paragraph are reasonable assumptions, then how strange it is that historians have experienced such difficulties in trying to explain what the objectives and goals of the American revolutionaries were; how strange that historians have contended so long and so bitterly about the motivations that propelled the revolutionaries to their tasks.

We know, of course, some of the reasons why historians are confused. They are human beings, and that in itself involves certain uncertainties. We know that the record of the past is seldom, if ever, complete, and that some men and women about whom we wish to know much left us almost no record of their actions, let alone their thoughts. And sometimes we feel uncomfortable with the words (even when we have them)—words like liberty, and freedom, which somehow seem too grandiose, or even masking of true motivations. We are troubled in our understanding of events of two centuries ago because eighteenth-century men and women were less likely than those who came after them to describe their emotional circumstances or environment. Records that we possess often seem too intellectualized, too devoid of emotional dimensions.

And historians have another concern. As David Potter once warned us, the participants in a historical situation tend to see alternatives in a less clear-cut, less sharply focused fashion than historians who come later, who look back and find shapes and patterns, dimensions and alternatives that might not have been at all clear to those involved in the historical situation.[1] Historians never will be able to fully understand, or precisely chronicle, the complex events of the American Revolution in the way it was understood by those who participated in it. But we keep trying, as is obvious tonight as I attempt to tell you what I think was in the minds of American women and men as they thought about, and made decisions concerning, the idea of American independence.

One of the Founding Fathers, John Adams, tempts us with his assertion that "the principles of the American Revolution may be said to have been as various as the thirteen states that went through it, and in some sense almost as diversified as the individuals who acted in it. In some few principles, or perhaps in one single principle, they all united."[2] With that as a challenge, we search through the records to see if we can find the principle or principles that Adams had in mind. You might think that, as they worked, historians would have come into ever greater agreement in their findings from that search. But that has not happened.

They have, instead, been very much divided. Some historians believe that the American Revolution was a political event, directed toward separating the American provinces from the British Empire, and that was all it was, no more than that—a political event. As Daniel J. Boorstin explains:

The most obvious peculiarity of our American Revolution is that, in the modern European sense of the word, it was hardly a revolution at all. The Daughters of the American Revolution, who have been understandably sensitive on this subject, have always insisted in their literature that the American Revolution was no revolution but merely a colonial rebellion. The more I have looked into the subject, the more convinced I have become of the wisdom of their naiveté.[3]

For those who share such views, political separation from Great Britain was the objective, the goal, the "essence" of the episode. The Revolution was a revolt against British rule, for American independence—period.

Another group of historians has argued otherwise. Their master-teacher, J. Franklin Jameson, pointed the direction a half-century ago, when he wrote:

The stream of revolution, once started, could not be confined within narrow banks, but spread abroad upon the land. Many economic desires, many social aspirations were set free by the political struggle, many aspects of colonial society profoundly altered by the forces thus let loose. The relations of social classes to each other, the institution of slavery, the system of land-holding, the course of business, the forms and spirit of the intellectual and religious life, all felt the transforming hand of revolution, all emerged from under it in shapes advanced many degrees nearer to those we know.[4]

To historians who follow Jameson, the American Revolution did not stop with political separation from the Mother Country. It was that, and in addition to that it was a liberalizing, unchaining event, going far beyond mere independence from the parent state.

Both groups of historians see special significance in the moment in which independence was declared. To the first (sometimes called Consensus) group, separation—or independence—*was* the American Revolution. Once Americans had decided that they should separate and that independence should be proclaimed, then the story of the American Revolution is only the story of how that independence actually was gained and recognized. To the other (termed the Progressive) historians, independence was the touchstone. Once it was decided upon, then the struggle to accomplish it generated subsidiary struggles as various groups and interests attempted to shape the economic, social, and intellectual institutions and patterns of American society.

So the idea of independence is central in all of the annals of and interpretations about the American Revolution. The components of that decision—the ingredients intermixed in the idea of independence—are what I wish to describe tonight.

The idea of independence as a concept to be acted upon probably was confronted by most American men and women sometime during the months from early in the year 1774 until midyear, 1776. We know that public discussion of the possibilities of separation from the Mother Country did not fully develop until January 1776, following publication of Thomas Paine's *Common Sense*. But we may well suppose that before that time many Americans privately considered the idea of independence. Theoretical, hypothetical predictions that at some future time Britain and America were destined to become separated had a very long history.[5] But independence as an idea for action is different, and my inquiry is directed to the idea as defined recently by Pauline Maier as focused on the time when the "colonists decided upon independence as an immediate goal and began to work toward it."[6]

As the Americans emerged out of the decade of debate over constitutional and economic policies with the Mother Country—from the Grenville legislation, especially the Stamp Act, through the Townshend difficulties, and into the Tea and other troubles of the 1770s—two distinct "paths" or "roads" opened before them. One of these we may label the Tory or Loyalist Road. It was the path that any American would follow if she or he was content with, and not disposed to argue about, relationships between America and Britain. Some of those who traveled this road were convinced that the provinces always would be—must be—part of the British Empire. Others were aware that relationships required mending, but would not have quarreled with the basic concept so emphatically stated by Parliament in the Declaratory legislation of 1766: we have the right "to bind the colonies and people of America, subjects of the Crown of Great Britain, in all cases whatsoever."

If you were on that road—the Tory Road—in the 1770s, you knew what the road led to, at least in its basic dimensions. The future, in its fundamental contours, would resemble the present, as the present resembled the past. There were no surprises, for the future already was discernible. Americans had been, were, and would continue to be subjects of the British Crown.

The other road open to Americans in those years should be termed the Whig Road. It was the pathway traveled by those colonists who believed that Americans had legitimate grievances against Great Britain and who attempted to find a way for forcing a redress of those grievances. The Tory Road, as shown in the diagram, ran in a straight line from the past, through the present, to the future. But the Whig Road had a fork in it. The past might be a common past, and the present a common present, but there were differing options for the future. One branch of the Whig roadway, as the diagram shows, ran from the fork to a goal or terminus labeled "reconciliation"; the other branch led toward an objective called "separation"—that is, independence.

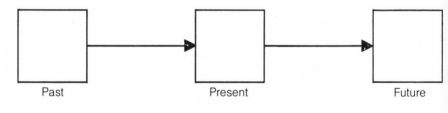

Past   Present   Future

THE TORY ROAD

To emphasize how very different were the circumstances characterizing the ends of those two branches of the Whig Road—separation, reconciliation—let me employ a somewhat crude, but I believe useful, analogy: Separation (Independence) as Divorce.

We grow up in our times using a metaphor eighteenth-century men and women used in their writing and speaking about British-American relationships—that of mother and children. While that metaphor is useful and historically valid, there are other analogies that also may help us understand the

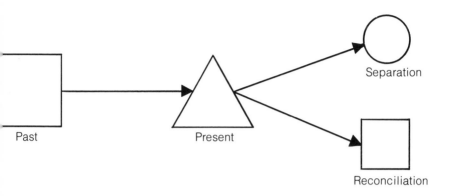

THE WHIG ROAD

past, for which, for the moment, accept the suggestion that what happened to Americans in 1776, in some ways, was like what happens to a partner in a marriage that is "going badly." The partners in this marriage, or at least one of them, hopes for reconciliation. One supposes that in such a situation, with reconciliation as the objective, then the goal (what is to result from the reconciliation) is to return to circumstances as they were at a more harmonious time in the marriage, some earlier time, perhaps the honeymoon days, when "things were going pretty good." The model of the future—the goal of the effort—then, is to return to circumstances already experienced—a future that is shaped like the past.

So Americans, traveling on the Whig Road and heading down the branch from the forks of that road toward reconciliation, could describe the future they hoped to attain quite simply by describing the past—that is, their relationships with the Mother Country before those relationships had become disarranged in the last decade.

On the other hand, consider divorce. The alternative, in this analogy, would occur when one of the marriage partners, or perhaps both of them, came to the conclusion that reconciliation was either impossible to attain or that the relationship had deteriorated so badly that the marriage was not worth trying to save. What then became the objective? Divorce—separation—independence. And with that as a goal, seriously thought of for the first time, all sorts of attendant questions come tumbling on—about how life will be structured and lived in strange and novel circumstances. Hopes and fears, anxieties and pleasures in contemplating the "new life" combine to produce a very different perspective of the future than that conjured with the goal of reconciliation.

So Americans, unhappy about their relationships with Britain, and eventually opting not for reconciliation when that no longer seemed possible, but, rather, for divorce, faced a future very different from the experienced past. All sorts of new vistas opened. The horizons of possibilities greatly expanded, as a mosaic of good and bad, hope and fear, old and new, tried and untried crowded contemplation.

In the years from 1774 to 1776, the road that branched into two forks—the Whig Road—changed in character. The branch leading toward reconciliation became narrower and narrower, more and more difficult to traverse, and finally, of course, it was barricaded against all travelers. What had seemed to be a viable passageway to recapture the past could not then be used. The travelers upon it had need to return to the fork in the road, to look down it toward independence and accept (however reluctantly) separation as the objective, or remove themselves from the Whig Road, seeking instead the Tory Road to follow to the future. So long as the branch leading toward reconciliation was open and traversable, then Americans had three options: the Tory Road, the Whig Road leading to reconciliation, and the Whig Road leading to independence. But when the reconciliation route was closed, then Americans were face to face with an either/or decision: either support and move forward toward independence, or reject that as providing an acceptable future.

To chose between those "futures," to confront fully the concept of a separate America, to entertain the "idea of independence" must have been a complicated individual dilemma. Emotional ties, psychological needs, many irrational elements undoubtedly contributed to each person's final decision. They were important, but so too were factors that were soberly, prudently, rationally analyzed by men and women.

As Americans weighed their future prospects, the components of the compound were commingled—hopes with fears, positive with negative assessments—comprising an amalgam in the thoughts of those who tried to construct a reasonably accurate prediction of the future of America.[7] Those who had sight only of the fearful aspects of an independent future probably already were determined anti-revolutionists. Those who could see only delight in their vision of an independent future surely would have been few (if any) in number. Most Americans had their hopes and fears combined. If the fears prevailed over the hopes, and they were pessimistic in their overall evaluation, then they probably sought the Tory Road. But if the hopes prevailed over the fears, and they were optimistic, then they would have supported independence.

The enumeration of the components that generated those hopes and fears surely would require a long list. Among the questions confronting Americans, these seem likely possibilities.

1. Can we win? Winning independence presumably would be more difficult than winning a negotiated reconciliation. These rational men and women were not likely to commit themselves to an effort that they believed was foredoomed to fail. Perhaps they did not engage in quite such a precise exercise as textbook writers do, when, in preparing to describe the War for American Independence, they draw a balance-sheet and assess the belligerents' relative advantages and disadvantages. Twentieth-century Americans have some difficulty in understanding how eighteenth-century Americans could have been optimistic in their assessment of their chances in armed conflict with Great Britain. Yet it does appear that sufficient numbers did believe that ultimate success on fields of battle— success enough to finally force a recognition of independence from the former parent state—was possible. One reason many Americans could believe that is because they had a ready answer to a second, somewhat dependent question.

2. Shall we seek and can we gain foreign aid? This really divides into two questions: "shall we seek foreign aid?" questioned the wisdom of the search; "can we gain foreign aid?" posited the possibility that it might not be attainable even though it was desirable to search for it. When Americans

thought about or talked about or acted toward gaining foreign aid they were thinking or talking or acting principally in reference to France. That was the most likely nation to see it in her self-interest to aid the Americans in rebellion against British rule. In fact, and then unknown to most Americans, France had decided to provide secret aid to the Americans.

For those who were primarily concerned with the first question (should we seek foreign aid?), the problem was the problem of "doing business with the old enemy." Catholic, monarchical France, for generations the enemy next door in Quebec, or Acadia, or the Ohio Country, was not and could not be imagined a friend to republican, Protestant, English-speaking Americans. If French aid, contaminated as it was, was sought, won, and accepted, then America would be opening herself to a mortgaged future. Take aid from France, it was argued, and you become her pawn. You may escape dependence upon Britain only to become dependent upon the old enemy. What sort of exchange was that?

Those who argued the other side insisted that France no longer was interested in mainland North American colonies, that her interest in America was only as a place to revenge herself against Britain and concurrently to secure a share of America's commerce. The colonies in America had made Great Britain a powerful nation (this was conventional wisdom in a mercantilist age); by cutting off the imperial connection. Britain's economic strength would dwindle, French economic strength would grow.

Furthermore, there was need to be quick in the decision on independence, for aid, trade, even alliance with France—and others—would come much sooner once the Americans had made manifest their determination to seek their independent national destiny. Carl Becker, in his essay "The Spirit of '76," effectively described the equations when his reluctant rebel, Jeremiah Wynkoop, related the chain of interrelated links: to have our rights we must fight; to fight we must have goods; to have goods we must have trade; to have trade we must have the support of France; to have the support of France we must declare our independence. "But will France aid us so long as we profess our loyalty to Britain? France will give money and troops to disrupt the British empire, but none to consolidate it. The act of separation will be the price of a French alliance."[8] For those less negative in their thoughts about separation, the final equation might be reversed to read: "A French alliance will be the reward for declaring independence."

3. Can the Americans remain united in their common cause? There was little difference of opinion as to the necessity of unity. Those who favored independence, and those who preferred to delay its declaration, and those who eventually opposed independence—all agreed that unity was essential. However, there was considerable disputation as to whether independence should come before or after the creation of formal unifying structures (articles of confederation) and about the difficulties impeding unity.

Among the arguments articulated by those persons who believed that union of interests was unlikely to be achieved, these statements might have been asserted: We are too different, as peoples, to share common goals. Our economies vary greatly as we are geographically different in our locations, from the Maine province of Massachusetts Bay in the Northeast to Georgia in the South. We are different in our religions. And we already are competing rivals on matters involving western lands and concerning common boundaries between us. Some of us are contesting with others over land grants in what will be Vermont; others over the Susquehanna Valley where Connecticut and Pennyslvania people both claim title to lands; and others in the Fort Pitt and Kentucky regions, where various interests collide. These, and many other divisive elements and issues, preclude unity among Americans.

On the other hand, Americans who were optimistic about their ability to continue in the common effort identified two existing, functioning instruments as symbolic of what could be accomplished: the Continental Congress and the Continental Army. Despite all the religious and economic differences among the states, and despite their competing rivalries over boundaries and lands, the states had generally supported the enactments and requests of the Congress. Similarly, the

"Common Cause" now was defended by an army maintained and directed by that Congress. Surely these were significant indications of functional unity.

4. Can America survive economically as an independent nation? There were worries about the lack of experience in manufacturing and concerns about cutting loose from traditional, imperial commercial habits and customs. But there also were optimistic assessments of what the American states could become if restraints imposed by Great Britain were removed, and Americans were free to seek markets in a wider world.

5. Will independence lead to disintegration of society? Those who made the American Revolution and those who opposed what they were doing both seem to have been concerned about social disintegration, the loosening of the bonds that tied society together. The people who were most pessimistic about the matter believed that they already had witnessed (in the advance of "new" men, "rough" men, demagogues) the beginnings of the dissolution of society they had known, and the creation of a new society in which they saw much to fear, even to loath. Many expressed this attitude, each in his own way, but perhaps none more directly than New Yorker Samuel Seabury who said: "If I must be enslaved, let it be by a king at least, and not by a parcel of upstart lawless committeemen. If I must be devoured, let me be devoured by the jaws of a lion, and not gnawed to death by rats and vermin."[9]

Others believed that society was disintegrating, or threatened to, not because of "new" men or "rough" men or demagogues, but because independence *had not yet been declared.* They pointed to the vacuum created by departing royal governors and governments, and the need to act quickly to structure legitimate governments in their place. These conditions seemed ample evidence to support a declaration of separation as America's goal. What the new governments were to be was republican governments—and many Americans were confident they would work. They saw independence as an affirmation of their belief in the ability of Americans to fashion governments that were more promising, more pure, than the corrupt, monarchical government Britain offered. And, persuaded that Americans could arrest the tendencies toward social disintegration, these people generally were optimistic about the future.

6. What was the future likely to be? While some men feared the result of social reordering, and saw dangers in the inevitable shifts in personal relationships, or anticipated general social instability from such change, others saw independence as ushering in the dawn of a new era, when Americans could rid their society of the excesses that conspiratorial designers from sin-ridden Britain would have fastened upon them. Now there might be realization of a model republic that would stand as a challenge to the rest of the world. Many men recorded that sense of challenge and destiny; among them was General Charles Lee who, writing to Governor Patrick Henry of Virginia, asserted:

I us'd to regret not being thrown into the World in the glorious third or fourth century of the Romans; but now I am thoroughly reconcil'd to my lot: the reveries which have frequently for a while serv'd to tickle my imagination . . . at length bid fair for being realiz'd. We shall now, most probably, see a mighty empire establish'd of Freemen whose honour, property and military glories are not to be at the disposal of a scepter'd knave, thief, fool, or Coward; nor their consciences to be fetter'd by a proud domineering Hierarchy—every faculty of the soul will now be put in motion—no merit can lye latent; the highest officers of the State both civil and military will now be obtain'd without court favour, or the rascally talents of servility and observance by which Court favour cou'd alone be acquir'd—sense, valour and industry, will conduct us to the goal; every spark of ability which every individual possesses, will now be brought forth and form the common aggregate for the advantage and honor of the Community.[10]

By asking these numbered questions about the idea of independence, unfortunately I've suggested too much structure (even symmetry) in the idea of independence. Few men would have decided to accept or acquiesce in all the negative, or all the affirmative, postures I've described. And, as I indicated earlier, in addition to such rational analysis, emotional and irrational forces also percolated through that society.

But I do believe that for the "cutting edge"—those persons who might be called the responsible minority among those who made the Revolution—some thoughts such as I have indicated in the questions probably did require responses. And in their assessments, leading to those responses, the optimists, the yea-sayers, prevailed as leaders over the pessimists, the nay-sayers. So far as history provides verdicts, they were right. The War for American Independence was a long and costly war, but the Americans did triumph, and those who said they could were proved as prophets. The French alliance created enormous problems for the young Republic, but it also provided significant aid to the American cause. Union among the American states and people was very difficult to maintain, but it was established sufficiently to keep the parts from flying in all directions, and a commonness of cause was nurtured sufficient to attend the birth of the Republic. Trade revived, manufacturing slowly increased, society did not disintegrate. And republican forms and virtues did provide the model, not only for America, but for much of the rest of the world as well.

4

Jack P. Greene

THE AMERICAN REVOLUTION: AN EXPLANATION

Two hundred years after the event, historians still do not have a clear answer to the great question of why the American Revolution, why, after a decade of relatively tempered and largely peaceful, if also firm, protest against certain specific measures and policies of the parent state, the American colonists suddenly took up arms, rose in rebellion, and rejected any further political association with that state? To put the question more specifically, what transformed that cautious and studied defiance still exhibited by the First Continental Congress in 1774 into the intense militancy of mid-1775 and the bitter revulsion against Britain during the first half of 1776?

There is, of course, a simple and obvious answer: the determination of the British government to use force to secure colonial obedience to its authority and the consequent outbreak of hostilities at Lexington and Concord on April 19, 1775. But such an answer only raises larger questions. Why did the British reach a determination to use force? Why did the Americans resist it? What gave the Americans any hope that their resistance, against the strongest power in the western world at that moment, might actually meet with success? These questions, in turn, raise still others. After they have happened, great events such as the American Revolution tend to take on an aura of inevitability. The "logic" of the event becomes so clear that it is difficult to entertain the possibility that it might not have happened at all. But only by understanding under what conditions the Revolution might *not* have occurred or the related question of why it did not occur earlier can we ever hope to understand the larger problem of how political protest escalated into armed rebellion and political revolution.

Any satisfactory examination of this problem must go back at least two decades to consider the nature of the bond that had held Britain and the colonies together for more than 150 years after the founding of the colonies.[1] The character of that bond is clearly revealed in the following four quotations.

The first dates from 1757 and is from Governor Thomas Pownall of Massachusetts Bay. Mocking the charge, made increasingly by people in Britain during the middle decades of the eighteenth century, that "in some future time the [American] Provinces should become Independent of the Mother Country," Pownall observed: "If by becoming Independent is meant a Revolt, nothing is further from their Nature, their Interest, their Thoughts; their Liberty & Religion is [sic] incompatible with French Government, and the only thing that the French could throw as a temptation in their way, namely, a *Free Port* is no more than they do enjoy now as their Trade is at present Circumstanced. They could hope for no Protection under a Dutch Government, and a Spanish cou'd give them neither the one nor the Other." "If," on the other hand, Pownall continued, "a Defection from the Alliance of the Mother Country be suggested, That their Spirit abhors, Their Attachment to the Alliance of the Mother Country is inviolable, Their Attachment to the Protestant Succession in the House of Hanover will ever Stand unshaken, *Nothing can eradicate these Attachments from their Hearts.*"[2]

The second is from Thomas Barnard, pastor of the First Congregational Church in Salem, Massachusetts. In a sermon celebrating the conclusion of the Seven Years' War in 1763, Barnard declared:

Now commences the Aera of our quiet Enjoyment of those Liberties, which our Fathers purchased with the Toil of their whole Lives, their Treasure, their Blood. Safe from the Enemy of the Wilderness [the Indians], safe from the griping Hand of arbitrary Sway and cruel Superstition [the French]; Here shall be the late founded Seat of Peace and Freedom. Here shall our indulgent Mother, who has most generously rescued and protected us, be served and honoured by growing Numbers, with all Duty, Love and Gratitude, till Time shall be no more.[3]

The third quotation is from Daniel Leonard, the articulate Massachusetts loyalist and lawyer. Writing on the very eve of the outbreak of war in the colonies in 1775, Leonard surveyed the crisis that then beset the British Empire with amazement:

When we reflect upon the constitutional connection between Great-Britain and the colonies, view the reciprocation of interest, consider that the welfare of Britain in some measure, and the prosperity of America wholly depends upon that connection, it is astonishing, indeed almost incredible, that one person should be found on either side of the Atlantic, so base and destitute of every sentiment of justice, as to attempt to destroy or weaken it. If there are none such, in the name of Almighty God, let me ask, wherefore is rebellion, that implacable fiend to society, suffered to rear its ghastly front among us, blasting with haggard look, each social joy, and embitttering every hour?[4]

The fourth and last quotation is from the patron philosopher of so many of the men of the Revolution, John Locke. In commenting in his *Second Treatise of Government* on the supposed susceptibility of governments founded on the will of the people to revolt and tumult, Locke made the sage observation that:

People are not so easily got out of their old Forms, as some are apt to suggest. They are hardly to be prevailed with to amend the acknowledg'd Faults, in the Frame they have been accustom'd to. And if there be any Original defects, or adventitious ones introduced by time, or corruption; 'tis not an easie thing to get them changed, even when all the World sees there is an opportunity for it. This slowness and aversion in the People to quit their old Constitutions, has, in the many Revolutions which have been seen in this Kingdom, in this and former Ages, still kept us to, or, after some interval of fruitless attempts, still brought us back again to our old Legislative of King, Lords and Commons.[5]

Together, these four quotations can help us to delineate the *ingredients of British imperial success* during Britain's first century and a half of empire. Locke's penetrating remarks remind us how very addicted people in traditional societies become to what Thomas Jefferson, paraphrasing Locke, referred to in the Declaration of Independence as "the forms to which they are accustomed,"[6] and how extraordinarily wary under *any* circumstances they are of *any* fundamental political change. As Leonard's remarks underline, this deep aversion to change was reinforced by the reciprocal economic—not to mention the political—benefits of empire. Britain had certainly profited from the colonies, but as Leonard emphasizes, the colonists had also derived great economic benefits from the connection with Britain. Students of the navigation acts have traditionally asked how much those economic restrictions *cost* the colonies. Far more deserving of emphasis perhaps is the extraordinary extent to which the colonies had been able to prosper under that system and by the middle of the eighteenth century had actually developed a strong vested interest in maintaining their economic ties with it. As Barnard's and Pownall's words particularly point up, however, the colonists were tied to Britain not only by interest and habit but also by deep affection and attachment. It is almost impossible to overemphasize the strength of these bonds of allegiance and affection that tied the colonies to Britain.

These bonds had powerful symbolic and psychological roots. For the colonists, Britain was the source of political, cultural and moral authority: it was at once the repository of the sacred "order of symbols, of values and beliefs" which were thought to give structure and legitimation to the lives of all Englishmen in Britain and the colonies and the site of the institutions—the Crown, Parliament, and the courts—charged with the exemplification and protection of that order.[7] Equally important, the connection with Britain also served the colonies as a source of pride and self-esteem, as Barnard's exclamations so clearly underscore. To have even a small share in the achievements of Britain during the eighteenth century—in the internal civil achievements exemplified by the establishment of an orderly government that permitted extensive individual liberty following the Glorious Revolution and the external achievements represented by the enormous expansion of foreign trade and the victory over the French and Spanish in the Seven Years' War—was an exhilarating experience that heightened British patriotism in the colonies and strengthened still further the psychological bonds between the colonists and Britain. Unlike most modern empires, then, the British Empire, at least as it existed prior to 1760, was held together not by force and not by overwhelming coercive powers—indeed, Britain's coercive powers in the colonies prior to the Seven Years' War were notoriously weak—but the voluntary attachment of the colonists, an attachment rooted in strong ties of habit, interest, and, more important, affection.

Of course, this voluntary attachment of the colonists to Britain depended, we can now see, to a large extent upon a set of implicit expectations about imperial behavior toward the colonies. These expectations proceeded from the assumptions that it was the moral obligation of the *mother* country to provide nurturance and protection for the colonies. What nurturance and protection had come to mean to the colonists can be briefly summarized: first, that the imperial government would interfere as little as possible with their ability to pursue whatever purposeful economic activities seemed to them to be in their best interest; second, that it would respect the sanctity of the local self-governing institutions on which the colonists depended for the immediate protection of the property they had acquired as a result of those activities; and, third, that in its dealings with the colonies it would continue to manifest respect for all of those central imperatives of Anglo-American political culture that were thought by Englishmen everywhere to be essential for the preservation of liberty and property.[8]

Once we understand the nature and power of the bonds that tied the colonies to Britain, we can see more clearly why it took so long for those bonds to become sufficiently weak to permit the colonists to seek to sever them altogether. In most explanations of the American Revolution, two events—the Seven Years' War and the Stamp Act crisis—are justifiably accorded a position of prominence. For eight years prior to the war—from the end of the previous war in 1748, to be precise—British officials had been systematically trying to reinforce British political authority in the colonies. The simultaneous eruption of severe political disturbances in several colonies during the late 1740s and early 1750s activated deep-seated—and during these years often reiterated—fears in Britain that the colonies might, if not immediately restrained, eventually become independent.

The response of the British government was to seek to tighten imperial controls at every possible point. Operating primarily through executive orders, British officials moved to place colonial governors under very close restraints, subjected colonial legislation to a more thorough scrutiny than they had for many decades, and, through a variety of expedients, sought to achieve some balance of political power in the colonies by curtailing the authority of the colonial lower houses of assembly, the elected bodies which had been nibbling away at the prerogatives of royal and proprietary governors for over a century. By the mid-1750s, it had become clear that these efforts were only minimally effective, and an increasing number of British officials had become persuaded that Parliament itself would have to intervene before British authority in the colonies could be adequately restored.

But the need for colonial support against the French and Spanish during the Seven Years' War forced British officials to abandon this new policy beginning in 1755–56, and colonial behavior during the war only increased the conviction in London that British authority in the colonies was dangerously weak and in need of considerable augmentation. Throughout the war, aggressive lower houses openly used Britain's need for defense funds to pry still more power away from governors; many colonial traders flagrantly violated British trade laws by carrying on direct commerce with the enemy and avoiding payment of duties, in many cases with the implicit connivance of the colonial governments and even of imperial customs officials; and many of the colonial legislatures failed to comply with imperial requisitions for men and money for the war effort—even with the promise of reimbursement by Parliament.

The war experience thus reinforced London's preexisting fears of loss of control over the colonies. It deepened suspicions that the colonists harbored secret desires for independence and intensified the determination among people in power in Britain to overhaul the imperial system. As soon as the British and colonial armies had defeated the French in

Canada in 1759–60 and colonial support for the war effort was no longer vital, London authorities undertook a variety of new restrictive measures to bolster imperial authority over the colonies.[9] The impulse behind these measures was not new. The shift from a permissive to a restrictive policy, from the traditional reliance upon the colonists' affections and allegiance to Britain to a dependence upon the threat of coercion to keep the colonies bound closely to Britain, had already occurred during the critical years from 1748 to 1756. The new measures of 1759 to 1764 were merely a renewal and an extension of that earlier reform program.

But, and this is the importance of the Seven Years' War for the origins of the American Revolution, they were an extension within a significantly different—and far more fragile— context. The war had been a psychologically liberating and reinforcing experience for the colonists. That so much of the war was fought on American soil and that the British government made such an enormous effort to defend the colonies gave rise to an expanded sense of colonial self-importance. Moreover, the colonists had contributed a substantial amount of money and a significant number of men to the war effort. Virginia and Massachusetts, the two colonies that subsequently took the lead in the resistance, in particular had, in terms of liquid resources, virtually bankrupted themselves in voting men and money for the war. As the Massachusetts pamphleteer Oxenbridge Thacher later protested, the colonies had "been guilty of no undutiful behavior towards" Britain "but on the contrary have greatly increased her wealth and grandeur and in the . . . [Seven Years'] war" had "impoverished themselves in fighting her battles."[10]

For the colonists, the knowledge that they had made such an important contribution to so great a national cause increased the immediacy and the strength of their ties with Britain. The war thus produced a surge of British patriotism among the colonists and created among them heightened expectations for a larger role within the empire, a role that would raise the status of the colonies from dependence upon to at least a nearer equivalence with the Mother Country.[11] By contrast, the war left British officials with feelings of bitterness and resentment toward the colonists and a determination to put them to a proper state of dependence. Having incurred an enormous debt and a heavy tax burden in defense of the colonies and having had exaggerated reports of American opulence and low taxes, they regarded colonial smuggling, failures to comply with royal requests for defense funds, and other examples of noncompliance with imperial regulations during the war as evidence of extreme ingratitude that verged on disloyalty. Such recalcitrant behavior, London officials feared, might eventually rob Britain of the large investment it had made in protecting and securing the colonies during the war.

If the experience of the war caused the postwar expectations of men on opposite sides of the Atlantic to veer off in such sharply different directions, the war itself altered the very structure of the relationship between Britain and the colonies. The expulsion of the French and Spanish from eastern North America removed the need for the last essential material benefit the British had to offer the mainland colonies—protection against the French and Spanish—and thereby presumably eliminated a major, if by no means the most powerful, block that had helped to keep whatever fantasies the colonists may have had about equivalence and independence in an unconscious and unarticulated state.[12] Far more important, by destroying French power in North America and thus making it less necessary to pacify the colonists, the British victory left subsequent British governments with a much freer hand to go ahead with their program of colonial reform. Moreover, for the first time, during and after the war, the British had a large number of royal troops in the colonies, 7,500 men in all.[13] By giving them an excessive confidence in their ability to suppress potential colonial opposition, the presence of these troops seems to have made British ministers less cautious and less concilatory in dealing with the colonies than they had been a decade earlier.

In combination, these psychological consequences and structural changes produced by the war made the relationship between Britain and the colonies much more volatile than it had been earlier. The colonists now had heightened expectations about their position in the empire and less need for Britain's protection, while British officials were bitter about colonial behavior during the war, more determined than ever to bring the colonies under closer control, persuaded that they would have to use the authority of Parliament to do so, and possessed of an army to back them up if it should be needed. Given this set of converging conditions, it was highly predictable that British officials in the 1760s would take some action, probably even by bringing Parliamentary authority to bear upon the colonies in new, unaccustomed, and hence, for the colonists, illegitimate ways that could be interpreted by the colonists as a fundamental violation of the existing relationship between them and Great Britain.

The colonial program of George Grenville did precisely that, and therein lies its principal importance for any understanding of the causes of the American Revolution. In 1763 and 1764, the American Revenue Act and various associated reforms sought to tighten British control over colonial shipping, curtail colonial smuggling, raise a revenue from American trade, and restrict colonial control over internal fiscal policy and western lands. In 1765, the Stamp Act threatened the colonies with still additional taxation. Direct Parliamentary taxation of the colonies was unprecedented, and this quick succession of measures seemed to the colonists to be an intolerable breach of traditional relationships within the empire. Along with the severe political crisis produced in the colonies by the Stamp Act, the Grenville measures did in fact profoundly alter the quality and character of imperial-colonial relations.

The first of the imperial reform measures to affect equally all of the colonies at once, the Stamp Act forced the colonists to identify more fully than ever before some of the major ambiguities and sources of strain within the imperial-colonial relationship as it had existed in the past. From the new perspective supplied by the Grenville program, they began to redefine their situation in a way that permitted them to interpret as grievances things that had previously gone unremarked and to perceive components of the earlier *ad hoc* imperial reform programs between 1748 and 1756 and between

1759 and 1764 as parts of a comprehensive assault upon the existing order that had been in progress for some time. This new perspective made the colonists hypersensitive to any subsequent violations or seeming violations of the existing order as they understood it.[14] The Stamp Act thus mobilized significant opposition in the colonies to Britain for the first time, and, even more important, opposition on the basis of a new definition of the colonial situation vis-à-vis recent British behavior. Morever, because the Stamp Act could be interpreted as at least a partial withdrawal of affection by the parent state, it permitted the colonists to articulate whatever preexisting hostile feelings they may have had toward Britain and thereby to legitimate aggressive actions against the imperial government. By thus weakening the ties of affection and allegiance the colonists had traditionally felt for Britain, the crisis over the Stamp Act began a process of erosion, what some political scientists have referred to as desacralization, of the traditional moral order within the old British Empire.[15]

For British political leaders, on the other hand, the intensity of colonial opposition to the Stamp Act only confirmed their long-standing suspicions that the colonists wanted nothing more than "to throw off all dependance and subjection."[16] The Stamp Act, declared Lord Sandwich, was "not the Object of their Sedition but to try their ground whether by Resistance they can get themselves loose from other Acts more disagreeable and detrimental to them." "The Americans," it appeared clearly, wanted "to get loose from the Act of Navigation" and all imperial political restraint.[17] How else could a community that was committed to the beliefs that Parliament was omnipotent and sovereignty indivisible interpret such an outrageous challenge to Parliamentary authority? The consequences of such a development were almost too abhorrent to contemplate. Separation of the colonies would inevitably mean, many people thought, that Britain would "dwindle and decline every day in our trade, whilst . . . [the colonists] thrive and prosper exceedingly" so that Britons would "run away as fast as they can from this country to that, and Old England" would "become a poor, deserted, deplorable kingdom."[18] Thus reduced to impotence and robbed of its power by its own children, Britain would ultimately "be Conquered in America & become a Province to her own Colonies."[19] Clearly, imperial authorities had been right in the impulse that had animated them since 1748: the colonies had to be brought under tighter control, imperial political authority had to be firmly and fully established.

The Grenville program and the Stamp Act crisis thus put a further strain upon a relationship already rendered fragile by the experience of the Seven Years' War and the imperial reform programs of 1748–56 and 1759–63. They combined to push the colonies into what modern systems theorists would call a *dysfunctional situation,* that is, a situation that was highly susceptible to disruption, breakdown, and malfunction. But a dysfunctional situation, however fragile, is not yet a *revolutionary situation.* The important analytical, and substantive, difference between a dysfunctional and a revolutionary situation—and the reason why the situation in the colonies did not become a revolutionary one for another nine years—was the presence of certain important deterrents, deterrents with sufficient power to forestall the complete breakdown of the imperial system, the emergence of a massive armed resistance, or even the development of a revolutionary movement bent upon changing the existing political order. Over the whole period from the repeal of the Stamp Act in 1766 until the outbreak of war at Lexington and Concord in April 1775, there were at least seven such deterrents.

First, and least important, was fear among colonial political leaders of loss of internal political control should British authority be removed. "We think ourselves happier . . . in being dependent on Great Britain, than in a state of independence," said an anonymous writer in the *New York Mercury* in 1764, "for then the disputes amongst ourselves would throw us into all the confusion, and bring on us all the calamities usually attendant on civil wars."[20] And, as Oliver Delancy of New York wrote his sister in England during the Stamp Act crisis, "should such unhappy Times come," the colonial elite would be extremely vulnerable to "the Ravages of the Populace" and "all [social] Distinction" would "then be lost . . . in such a scene of Confusion and Distress."[21] How many people held such fears

is not clear. Certainly, the willingness of many traditional political leaders to bring seamen, tradesmen, and laborers into
their protests against the Stamp Act and later measures
suggests not a fear of the populace but an extraordinary—if, as
we now know, somewhat misplaced—confidence in their ability to manipulate and control it. Yet the intensity of the Stamp
Act riots—especially the sacking of Lieutenant Governor
Thomas Hutchinson's house in Massachusetts and similar actions in some other colonies—did give the colonial political
elite concrete reasons to fear the uncontrolled wrath of an
aroused mob, reasons which were reinforced by some inci-
dents between 1767 and 1770 during the crisis over the
Townshend Acts.[22]

A corollary of this fear of loss of internal political control and
a second deterrent was a manifest lack of confidence in the
colonists' ability to fend for themselves in a hostile world.
"Exposed by our situation, by a rivalship and competition of
Interests, and yet in a state of infancy," said Joseph Reed in
1766, "it would be extremely difficult, if not impossible, to
form any Union among ourselves that would be sufficient to
repel the attacks of a formidable invader." Thus "to throw off
all dependence on the mother country" would only be to "put
themselves in the situation of a silly girl, who leaves the guid-
ance and protection of a wise and affectionate parent, and
wandering away exposes herself to ruin by the artful insinua-
tions of every wicked and designing stranger."[23] As the remarks of Governor Pownall quoted earlier illustrate, it was a
widespread belief that the colonies were too disunited and too
immature to make it on their own and that independence from
Britain would necessarily mean something far worse: domination by France, Spain, or the Netherlands, all of which had
established records of permitting colonies vastly less
freedom—in both the political and economic spheres—than
that allowed to the colonies by the British. And, given the
vaunted disunion of the colonies, the best that could be hoped
for, as John Dickinson, the famous Pennyslvania farmer, wrote
to William Pitt, was "a multitude of Commonwealths, Crimes
and Calamities—centuries of mutual Jealousies, Hatreds,
Wars and Devastations, till at last the exhausted Provinces shall

sink into Slavery under the yoke of some fortunate conqueror."[24]

A third and related deterrent was a deeply rooted fear of—and aversion to—republicanism as a form of government. The colonists, like Britons generally, had unhappy memories of the chaotic republican experiments in England during the English Revolution of 1640–60 and, as both Thomas Pownall's and Thomas Barnard's remarks indicated, they were deeply attached to the British variant of monarchical government. Moreover, the almost universal belief among political theorists in the eighteenth century was that republicanism was suitable only for very small political units like Geneva or Venice or the United Provinces of the Netherlands. However republican American society might actually appear to *be* to contemporary Englishmen,[25] republicanism, the only possible form of government for the colonies should they become independent, was, if not a frightening, certainly by no means an attractive prospect for virtually all colonial political leaders.[26] "A republican form of government," as one American loyalist later categorically declared, "would neither suit the genius of the people, nor the extent of America."[27]

The fourth deterrent was fear of British coercive power. There had always been a healthy respect for British power among the colonists, but such respect could only have been increased by the new military and naval presence in the colonies after 1756, a presence that for the first time in the continental colonies gave the British government significant coercive powers. How could the colonies, weak in liquid economic resources—the very sinews of war—and disunited, have any chance at all against such a mighty power? Clearly, to enter into martial combat with Britain would only be to court "Devastation and ruin" for the colonies.[28]

A fifth deterrent was the lack of political institutions capable of mounting and sustaining any generalized resistance movement. The disunion of the British continental colonies was notorious. In most cases, the connection of individual colonies with Britain was far more direct than it was with any other colony. The local lower houses of assembly in each colony could—and did—supply some leadership in any protest movement, but they could be—and were—frequently dissolved or not summoned at all because they depended for their legal authority upon some imperial charter or upon the governor's royal commissions. More important, perhaps, there was no central governing institution capable of providing the leadership necessary for a successful general opposition movement.

A sixth deterrent was what might best be called the British penchant for compromise, for finding a *political* solution to fundamental issues of conflict in the public sphere. The repeal of the Stamp Act in 1766 and the removal of all the Townshend duties except for a token tax on tea in 1770 were classic examples of the operation of this penchant. Both of these actions removed the major source of immediate contention and ignored the basic issues in dispute. In their relations with the colonies over the previous century, imperial authorities had repeatedly adopted this mode to the immediate mutual satisfaction and advantages of the parties concerned. The continued willingness of British officials to eschew the search for a *final* solution about such questions as Parliament's authority over the colonies in return for the immediate advantage of political tranquillity and the continuing economic benefits derived from the colonies always, as colonial behavior during the quiet period that obtained between repeal of the Townshend duties in 1770 and the renewal of contention in 1773 so powerfully attests, was a strong deterrent to revolution and a necessary precondition for the continued viability of the empire.

The seventh, last, and far and away the most important deterrent was the continuing power of the habitual ties of allegiance and affection felt for Britain by the colonists and the colonists' deep psychological dependence upon Britain. Sustained by the widespread illusion that the colonies had a large reservoir of political support in Britain, an illusion rooted in a fundamental misreading of both the motives behind ministerial and Parliamentary support for yielding to American demands during the Stamp Act and Townshend Acts crises and the influence of Wilkeite radicals and other pro-American groups in British political life,[29] those ties and that dependence were so strong—the residue of affection was so large—as to prevent most colonists, even in the face of a long chain of what they interpreted as serious violations of the traditional relationship between 1764 and 1774, from permitting any unconscious fantasies they may have had about equivalence and independence from becoming conscious wishes or goals and from allowing their resentment of British official behavior to become so great as to cause them to reject their connection with Britain.

It is the continuing force of these deterrents that explains why the Revolution did not occur earlier; to explain why the Revolution occurred when it did requires an examination of how these extraordinarily powerful deterrents were sufficiently weakened as to give so many colonists the heart and the nerve to rebel. A number of interrelated developments, first in the period between the repeal of the Stamp Act in 1766 and the passage of the Coercive Acts in early 1774 and then in the crucial period between the end of the First Continental Congress in the fall of 1774 and the Declaration of Independence in July 1776 are relevant to a consideration of this question.

A development of major importance in the earlier period was the gradual deflation of British power in the colonies as illustrated by the successful colonial defiance of, first, the Townshend measures, then, the Tea Act, and, finally, the Coercive Acts themselves. The ability of the colonies to defy these measures and, what is more important, the inability of British officials in the colonies to enforce them helped to weaken colonial respect for British coercive power and to encourage the suspicion that it might be successfully defied. On the other side, successful colonial defiance of Parliamentary measures left the British government with three clear choices. First, it might in the traditional manner seek to allay colonial opposition by making minor policy concessions. This is the course it followed to put an end both to the Stamp Act and to the Townshend Acts crises. Second, and this is what colonial leaders were demanding, it might undertake some structural rearrangements in the direction of increased colonial autonomy specifically designed to remove all long-term causes of colonial discontent. Third, it could remain essentially intransigent and seek to enforce its will by force.

Assuming that it could be successfully implemented, either the second or the third choice had the attraction of promising to put an end to the now seemingly perpetual discord between Britain and the colonies. But the second choice was never a legitimate option for the British political nation. It would have required not merely some conservative changes in institutional structure; it would also have required the acceptance of some form of multi-sovereignty within the empire, an arrangement that was unacceptable to the British government and had no support whatever within the British political nation because it was at direct variance with the basic British beliefs that sovereignty was indivisible and the authority of Parliament absolute.[30] The more Americans seemed to challenge these two beliefs—and they did so explicitly throughout the last half of 1774—the more tightly the British clung to them; the more fearful the British became of colonial independence, of the loss of control over the colonies and of the economic benefits they derived from the colonies; the less viable the first choice—of making further political concessions—seemed to be; and the more the British were pulled toward the third alternative of seeking a resolution to the controversy by enforcing British authority in the colonies at whatever costs. This was the course they adopted in rejecting Congress's appeals to remove the Coercive Acts. They were the more easily pulled in this direction by the general belief that the colonists could neither sustain a unified resistance—had not the non-importation movements of 1768–70 collapsed as public spirit had yielded to private interests?—nor put up an effective defense, a belief that was rooted in and reinforced by a deep, almost xenophobic contempt for the colonists' martial capabilities.

A second development of importance in weakening the many deterrents to revolution in the colonies was the increasing politicization of the colonies around a central focus of opposition to British policy. The controversy with Britain tended to draw an increasing number of people into political activity with the traditional elite being recruited first because it was the most Anglicized sector of the colonial population and presumably the most sensitive to imperial violations of traditional British values and the by now largely explicit structure of colonial expectations about the proper modes of imperial behavior toward the colonies. But most other segments of the population were recruited relatively easily, partly because British moral authority was presumably less strong with time to begin with and because they were—for reasons of ideology, habit, and in some cases, interest—accustomed to following the lead of the elite anyway.[31]

Corollaries of this process of political mobilization were: 1) the opening up of new career opportunities in politics and the attachment of higher status to political activity—in the great crisis after 1765 the road to fame was in the political arena rather than in religion or economic life;[32] 2) heightened political sensibilities throughout the politically relevant segments of society; and 3) the fixing of attention of a broad spectrum of colonial society firmly upon political questions involving the relationship between Britain and the colonies.[33] A final aspect of this increased politicization of colonial society was the routinization of collective violence to achieve political objectives. Each new crisis produced a greater resort to extralegal force, the burning of the British revenue cutter *Gaspee* in Rhode Island in 1772 and the Boston Tea Party in 1773 being only the most dramatic examples.[34] Very importantly, however, these extralegal and crowd actions were sufficiently controlled as to help persuade many colonial leaders that the removal of British authority would not automatically result in political anarchy in the colonies and to give the colonists increasing confidence in their capacity to govern themselves.

A third and related development—one that was critical in driving British authorities toward a less moderate stand—was the alienation of the overseas trading merchants, the colonists' main allies in Britain, by the adoption of agreements not to import goods from or export products to Britain first at the time of the Townshend Acts and again in response to the Coercive Acts. "The Americans have by this Measure lost many valuable Friends," wrote the Bristol merchant Richard Champion to a South Carolina correspondent in 1770. America, he said, "should have levelled her Resentment upon Administration, who really oppressed her, and not upon the Commercial and Manufacturing part of the Kingdom, who were always her best Friends."[35]

But by far the most important development was what might be called the gradual desacralization of the customary moral order that had always been the primary binding force between Britain and the colonies. This process was especially evident in the rapid spread and intensification of a generalized belief in the evil intentions of men in power in Britain and in the corruption of the central governing institutions of the empire. Such "a series of oppressions" as the British government had since the early 1760s "pursued unalterably through every change of ministers," declared Jefferson in the summer of 1774, "too plainly prove a deliberate and systematical plan of reducing us to slavery."[36] Through the end of 1774, however, the process was still incomplete. The colonists had moved from a belief in ministerial conspiracy to a conviction that Parliament was also corrupt. But they retained a great amount of respect for the king and for the essential justice and virtue of the British people. The growing belief in ministerial and Parliamentary corruption had however permitted a gradual lapse of the repressions that had previously prevented the articulation and internalization of aggressive feelings toward Britain. Moreover, during the crisis over the Townshend Acts and after, resistance to British corruption came to be seen as the best way to purge colonial society of its own inner stains as they were becoming disturbingly manifest in excessive consumerism and self-oriented behavior. Self-denial—through the nonconsumption of British goods—was envisioned as the best possible way of recalling the colonists to the industrious, frugal, and virtuous ways of their ancestors. Opposition to Britain and the purification of colonial society were thus explicitly coupled.[37]

Each of these developments—the deflation of British power with a growing predisposition to use force to seek a final resolution of the colonial problem, the increasing politicization of the colonies, the alienation of the colonists' primary friends in Britain, and the gradual desacralization of the customary and binding moral order—helped to undermine the main deterrents to revolution between 1766 and 1774. But it was only as a result of the crisis engendered by the Tea Act of 1773, the colonial response to it, and the Coercive Acts of 1774 that those deterrents were sufficiently weakened to convert the highly fragile or dysfunctional situation into a potentially revolutionary one. There were several critical developments in this process.

First, from the colonial point of view, the Coercive Acts themselves and the chain of events that followed could be—and were—interpreted as new and fundamental violations of the customary moral order that bound the colonies to Britain. Such blatant violations were those measures that they seemed to leave no doubt, as Ebenezer Baldwin, Congregational pastor at Danbury, Connecticut, declared, that the British ministry was indeed pursuing that "settled fixed plan . . . for *inslaving* the colonies" that many colonists had come more and more to suspect over the previous decade had been at the root of their difficulties with the imperial government. This growing conviction that submission would lead to "a state of abject slavery"[38] gave rise not only to a broadly diffused determination to resist the Coercive Acts even if it meant taking up arms—a completely new level of militancy that was signified and given semiofficial sanction with the adoption in September 1774 by the First Continental Congress of the Suffolk Resolutions advising the inhabitants of beleaguered Massachusetts to arm themselves. This conviction also resulted in a sharply articulated and widely generalized belief among a large segment of the colonial political community that fundamental changes in the traditional structure of the empire were absolutely necessary if the colonists were ever to be secure in their liberty, property, and fundamental life goals. As North Carolina instructed its delegates to the First Continental Congress, the colonists required not only the removal of existing grievances but a clear statement "*with certainty*" of "the rights of Americans"[39] and, said the Rhode Island instructions, "proper measures . . . to establish" those "rights and liberties of the Colonies, upon a just and solid foundation."[40] For only when that was done, experience from the perspective of the many "assaults upon American liberty" over the last decade seemed to indicate, would the colonists have that security of liberty and property that was the indispensable precondition for the restoration, in the words of the New Hampshire credentials, of "that peace, harmony, [and] mutual confidence which once happily subsisted between the parent country and her Colonies."[41] Nor was this a parochial matter. At issue, said Eliphalet Dyer, a Connecticut delegate to the Congress, was nothing less than "the liberties of the West Indies and of the people of Great Britain, as well as our own, and perhaps of Europe."[42] The stakes could scarcely have been higher nor the determination not to give in until proper safeguards had been achieved any greater.

Escalating militancy in the colonies was met by mounting intransigence in Britain, where the extremity of the colonial position cost the colonists most of their remaining friends in British political life. Temporizing in the face of such a blatant challenge to British authority, British leaders believed, would only mean what so many Britons had all along feared and what in an effort to avoid it had initially set in motion the long chain of actions that Americans had found so objectionable: that is, the certain loss of the colonies. And the loss of the colonies, most British writers thought despite demurs from economists like Adam Smith and Josiah Tucker, could only mean that Britain would "sink for want of trade" as "a new empire America controuls all Europe."[43] Such fears were behind the fateful decision by imperial authorities in late 1774 and early 1775 to use force if necessary to secure colonial obedience to Parliamentary authority.

It was the actual use of force beginning at Lexington and Concord and the subsequent clash of arms, however, that, more than anything else, completed the destruction of British moral authority in the colonies and encouraged the expression of previously repressed and unacceptable militant feelings toward Britain—so evident in the bitter outpourings against Britain and the hostile treatment of those colonists who could not or did not oppose Britain—as well as hitherto unconscious fantasies about independence, which were brought into the open following publication of Thomas Paine's *Common Sense* in early 1776.[44] Once expressed, these aggressions and fantasies formed a new basis for the evaluation of the traditional imperial-colonial relationship, an evaluation that permitted the consideration of what had previously been impossible to consider: the desirability of monarchy and of the connection with Britain. Once these previously illegitimate ideas had been rendered legitimate by the collapse of British moral authority in the colonies and the conversion of colonial affection for Britain into abject dislike during the summer and fall of 1775, the colonists found themselves, for the first time, in a genuinely revolutionary situation.

If the collapse of British moral authority and the consequent alienation of colonial affections were the primary ingredients in the movement of the controversy into a revolutionary state, other developments during 1774 and 1775 removed still other deterrents. To begin with, the course of the war during its first year helped to encourage the colonists in the belief that they might successfully oppose the coercive might of Great Britain as long as they stuck together, especially given the vastness of the colonies with the consequent difficulties of conquest and the ever increasing likelihood of assistance from France.

In addition, Congress supplied the colonies for the first time with an agency capable of directing and sustaining unified political resistance, while the provincial congresses at the colony level and the committees of safety at the local level provided them with local governing institutions not dependent for their legal authority upon Britain. These proto-republican institutions provided reasonably coordinated leadership of the resistance; more important, their successful functioning helped both to allay fears that the removal of British authority would lead to political collapse in the colonies and to demonstrate the viability of republican government.[45] In fact, the prospect of creating successful republican governments for the colonies came increasingly to be seen as a great and formidable challenge, a once-in-history opportunity that might serve as an example for the rest of mankind—who, said the British radical philosopher Dr. Richard Price, mostly still lived in "ignominious slavery"[46]—at the same time that it managed to restrain power and luxury and promote liberty and virtue in the colonies.

For a significant and respectable segment of Americans, of course, Britain continued to retain much of its old moral authority, British military and naval power its old awe, and the prospect of life without the superintending power of Britain its old fears. They were the anti-revolutionaries or the non-revolutionaries who found the prospect of independence, republicanism, and government under the leaders of colonial resistance far more frightening than the continuation of the traditional connection with Britain, albeit most of these men believed with the First Continental Congress that that connection ought to be based on strict guarantees of American liberty and property.[47] For the leaders of the resistance, however, nothing could be more frightening than the prospect of a continued connection with a degenerate Britain unable to resist the tyrannical schemes of a power-hungry king and his minions in administration and Parliament.

The colonists had not come to this conclusion lightly or quickly. On the contrary, their course of behavior had been accurately predicted by John Locke in a paragraph following the one quoted earlier. *"Revolutions,"* said Locke,

happen not upon every little mismanagement in publick affairs. *Great mistakes* in the ruling part, many wrong and inconvenient Laws, and all the *slips* of humane frailty will be *born by the People,* without mutiny or murmur. But if a long train of Abuses, Prevarications, and Artifices, all tending the same way, make the design visible to the People, and they cannot but feel, what they lie under, and see, whither they are going; 'tis not to be wonder'd, that they should rouze themselves, and endeavour to put the rule into such hands, which may secure to them the ends for which Government was at first erected; and without which, ancient Names, and spacious Forms, are so far from being better, that they are much worse, than the state of Nature, or pure Anarchy; the inconveniences being all as great and as near, but the remedy farther off and more difficult.[48]

It was just such a long chain of apparent abuses that primarily explained to colonial leaders of the resistance why they were justified, nay, *compelled,* to reject the old order and why they could take solace in their belief that the governments they would create would be the only remaining legitimate embodiments of what—and it was much—was worth preserving in that order.

Insofar as it is desirable or permissible to talk about *the sufficient* cause of any event so complex as the American Revolution, one would thus have to turn to the British effort at colonial reform beginning in 1748 and the long series of abuses that it represented to so many colonists. These "abuses" eventuated in the slow erosion of British moral authority in the colonies, the gradual loss of confidence in Britain's capacity to provide satisfactory government for the colonies, and the tortured alienation of the strong affections the colonists had originally held for Britain—an alienation that itself ran so deep as to persuade the leaders of colonial resistance that not even the awesome power of Britain, the unhappy history of republican governments, their own notorious disunion, or the few remaining friends they had in Britain, could deter them from seeking to break off all further connections.

5

James Morton Smith

JOHN ADAMS AND THE COMING OF THE REVOLUTION

On October 3, 1961, I drove up from Williamsburg, Virginia, to Washington, D.C., to attend a luncheon sponsored by the *Washington Post* to mark the publication of the first four volumes of The Adams Papers, and to see for the first time the new president of the United States, John F. Kennedy. Both President Kennedy and President Adams were from Massachusetts and Mr. Thomas B. Adams, John's great-great-great grandson, also from Massachusetts, attended this luncheon as president of the Massachusetts Historical Society. Since John and Abigail Adams were the first First Family to live in the White House, President Kennedy turned to Mr. Thomas B. Adams and said: "First of all, I want to say to Mr. Adams, that it is a pleasure to live in your family's old house, and we [Jackie and I] hope that you will come by and see us." Then President Kennedy turned to President Adams and the Revolutionary generation:

[A]ll of us as Americans are constantly bemused and astounded by this extraordinary golden age in our history which produced so many men of exceptional talent. I have not heard, nor I suppose is there a rational explanation for the fact that this small country, possessed of a very limited population, living under harsh circumstances, produced so many . . . brilliant and extraordinary figures who set the tone for our national life and who really represent the most extraordinary outpouring of human ability devoted to government, . . . than any time since the days of Greece. And any touch which we may have in our lives with that period attracts us all.[1]

The Bicentennial, if it does nothing more than bring us in

75

touch with that golden age and with those extraordinary and brilliant men who set the tone for our national life, will be a considerable success. And surely one of the most brilliant of that brilliant galaxy of the Revolutionary era was Mr. Kennedy's compatriot from Massachusetts, John Adams. Yet Adams has never been as popular a figure among Americans as his Revolutionary colleagues, President George Washington, who preceded him, and Thomas Jefferson, who followed him as president. Why should that be?

John Adams himself had a ready answer. "Popularity was never my Mistress," he wrote to his friend James Warren in 1787. "Nor was I ever, or shall I ever be a popular Man."[2] "Mausoleums, statues, monuments will never be erected to me," Adams wrote after his retirement from the presidency. "I wish them not. Panegyrical romances will never be written, nor flattering orations spoken to transmit me to posterity in brilliant colors."[3] That prediction has remained essentially correct.

But if popularity was not his goal, fame was. "Reputation," he noted as a young lawyer, "ought to be the perpetual subject of my Thoughts, and Aim of my Behaviour. How shall I gain a Reputation! How shall I Spread an Opinion of myself as a Lawyer of distinguished Genius, Learning, and Virtue." He concluded that he should "look out for a Cause to Speak to, and exert all the Soul and all the Body I own, to cut a flash, strike an amazement, to catch the vulgar." Weighing "a bold Push, a resolute attempt, a determined Enterprize" against "a slow, silent, imperceptible creeping," he decided in favor of "some uncommon unexpected Enterprize in Law. . . . [I] will strike with surprize—surprize Bench, Bar, Jury, Auditors and all." And he noted, "[I'll] have some Boon, in Return, Exchange, fame, fortune, or something."[4] Throughout his long life John Adams aimed at, and struggled for, greatness, for solid and lasting fame, for approbation of his services to state and society.

If popularity escaped him, greatness did not. But fame did not come at once and perhaps its coming at all surprised no one more than John Adams, for Adams was almost always his own severest critic. He was, as Lyman Butterfield, the editor of The

Adams Papers has observed, "a relentlessly keen and candid observer of himself,"[5] and it is this very openness and candor that makes Adams so appealing to the modern reader. He not only recorded his innermost hopes and ambitions, but he also castigated his jealousness, passions, and naïveté, his languor, sloth, negligence, his "faults, Defects, Fopperies and Follies, and Disadvantages," and his inordinate vanity.[6] Indeed, Edmund S. Morgan of Yale University has characterized Adams's *Diary and Autobiography* "as the culminating volumes of the history of vanity in New England."[7] And Clinton Rossiter of Cornell University has observed that Adams "wore the scratchiest hair shirt over the thinnest skin in American history."[8]

But there was in Adams a constructive tension between being vain and seeking fame, for at the same time that he urged himself forward most vigorously in pursuit of "fame, fortune, or something," he noted that success would not come from "Fortune, Fame, Beauty, Praise, and all such Things" but only from "an habitual Contempt" of them.[9] "The Love of Fame," he wrote at the age of twenty, is a passion that "is apt to betray men into impertinent Exertions of their Talents, sometimes into censorious Remarks upon others, often into little meannesses to sound the opinions of others and oftenest of all into a childish Affection of Wit and Gaiety. I must own my self to have been, to a very heinous Degree, guilty in this Respect." "No Virtues," he concluded, "are a sufficient Attonement for Vanity."[10]

The key to Adams's character and career lies in his Puritan upbringing and his early training for the ministry. The first-born son of Deacon John Adams and Susanna Boylston, young John grew up acknowledging and practicing a strict Puritan morality. Long before he decided at the age of twenty-one to study law, his views of life, work, and the world were firmly formed. "God has told us," he wrote,

that This World was not designed for a lasting and a happy State, but rather for a State of moral Discipline, that we might have a fair Opportunity and continual Excitement to labour after a cheerful Resignation to all the Events of Providence, after Habits of Virtue, Self Government, and Piety. And this Temper of mind is in our Power to acquire, and this alone can secure us against all the Adversities of Fortune, against all the Malice of men, against all the Opperations of Nature.[11]

Always noted as an advocate of checks and balances—whether in government or in harnessing the passions of mind and soul, he constantly struggled as a young man—and indeed, throughout life—to check passion with reason, freedom with responsibility, and to weigh pleasure against pain, conveniences against inconveniences. At the age of twenty he scribbled into his diary the observation that

he is not a wise man and is unfit to fill any important Station in Society, that has left one Passion in his Soul unsubdued. . . . [Avarice, Love, Envy are passions that] should be bound fast and brought under the Yoke. . . . But properly inured to Obedience, they take their Places under the Yoke without Noise and labour vigorously in their masters Service. From a sense of the Government of God, and a Regard to the Laws established by his Providence, should all our Actions for ourselves or for other men, primarily originate. And This master Passion in a good mans soul, like the larger Fishes of Prey will swallow up and destroy all the rest.[12]

In striving to be a good man, Adams carefully monitored his own conduct, constantly measuring performance against promise, achievement against aspiration. He was full of good intentions and resolutions:

I am resolved to rise with the Sun and to study the Scriptures, on Thursday, Fryday, Saturday, and Sunday mornings, and to study some Latin author the other 3 mornings. Noons and Nights I intend to read English Authors. . . . I will rouse up my mind, and fix my Attention. I will stand collected within my self and think upon what I read and what I see. I will strive with all my soul to be something more than Persons who have had less Advantages than myself.[13]

"May I blush," he concluded on another occasion, "whenever I suffer one hour to pass unimproved."[14]

The young Adams must have blushed a lot, for his diary is filled with self-admonitions, lamentations over his backsliding, and exhortations to improvement. "I know not by what Fatality it happens," he complained at twenty-two, "but I seem to have a Necessity upon me of trifling away my Time."[15] On another occasion he meticulously listed the many different ways he had frittered away his time:

> I have smoaked, chatted, trifled, loitered away this whole day almost. By much the greatest Part of this day has been spent, in unloading a Cart, in cutting oven Wood, in making and recruiting my own fire, in eating nuts and apples, in drinking tea, cutting and smoaking Tobacco and in chatting with the Doctor's Wife [Mrs. Elisha Savil] at their House and at this. Chores, Chatt, Tobacco, Tea, Steal away Time.[16]

And, he resolved anew to spend his time more profitably. But, predictably, there were other self-critical notations, including a marvelous self-castigation for a four-day period spent "in absolute Idleness, or what is worse, gallanting the Girls."[17]

If idleness was the devil's workshop, John Adams had innumerable opportunities to get reasonably well acquainted with the devil. But if work was the enemy of that devil vanity, then Adams also labored diligently to banish the devil and subjugate the enemy, as his early diary and his later autobiography so clearly reveal. Even when he forsook heavenly for worldly glory by switching from divinity study to the law, Adams continued to abhor idleness and luxury. In short, he was more interested in fame "or something" than in fortune. When Jeremiah Gridley, the leading lawyer of Massachusetts Bay Colony, agreed to sponsor Adams before the bar, he advised him to "pursue the Study of the Law rather than the Gain of it. Pursue the Gain of it enough to keep out of the Briars, but give your main Attention to the study of it."[18] Gridley's advice confirmed the already fixed views of Adams, who was critical of moneygrubbers. Only a week before he had blasted Dr. Elisha Savil for his most prevalent passion, "the desire of Money. . . . He aims not at fame," Adams wrote contemptuously, but "only at a Living and a fortune!"[19]

Although Adams left the study of the ministry with some reluctance—"My Inclination I think was to preach," he wrote—he carried over his Puritanical views to the law. "The Study and Practice of Law," he reassured himself, "does not dissolve the obligations of morality or of Religion." And he added that he had made firm resolutions "never to commit any meanness or injustice in the Practice of Law."[20] It was the law and a career in public service that finally propelled Adams to fame. And it was the Revolution that opened first a national and then an international arena for his talents and his ambition. For as eager as he was to win the plaudits of those around him, he never lost sight of the brighter glory of Massachusetts's rights—both civil and religious—of national independence, or of personal and political integrity.

Despite his view of himself as a frivolous soul, John completed his legal studies before he was twenty-three. After being admitted to the Massachusetts bar in November 1758, Adams practiced in his hometown of Braintree. In his early years, his legal business grew steadily, as did his stature in the community. In recognition of his standing, the Braintree town meeting elected him Surveyor of Highways in 1761. In the fall of 1762, the twenty-seven year old lawyer began a serious courtship with Abigail Smith, a woman nine years his junior, whom he had known since 1759. Busily improving the farm he loved, John brought Abigail Smith there as his wife in October 1764. In temperament, character, and intelligence, the remarkable Abigail was a singularly perfect partner for John Adams.

Marriage settled Adams greatly. Although he continued to fuss about his reputation and future, he was no longer quite so plagued with restlessness and morbidity as previously. In January 1765, he accepted an invitation to join a select group of Boston lawyers in the "Sodality," a lawyer's club for reading and discussing the law. The invitation signified Adams's acceptance as a rising young lawyer with a promising future; the club itself gave him an opportunity to develop his ideas and discuss them with others.

Adams's training in the Sodality prepared him for the decade of controversy between 1765 and 1775 over the right of Parliament to tax the American colonies. The Stamp Act of 1765 was Parliament's first attempt to tax the American colonies, and the explosive colonial response revealed the gulf between imperial theory and colonial practice, for it pitted inalienable right against absolute power. Parliament claimed that by its sovereign power it could adopt acts which no earthly power could undo.

And the colonists argued that there were fundamental

rights which no government, no matter how powerful, could deprive them of. This was Adams's line of argument in his first paper prepared for the Sodality Club, "A Dissertation on the Canon and Feudal Law." Emphasizing that an assertion of the people's rights, which were "antecedent to all earthly government," could redress governmental wrongs, Adams became a spokesman for "the liberty side" against "the prerogative side" in Massachusetts. America, he wrote, had been peopled by those seeking civil as well as religious liberty: "it was a love of universal liberty, and a hatred, a dread, a horror, of the infernal confederacy [of the tyranny of canon and feudal law] that projected, conducted, and accomplished the settlement of America," he wrote. "Tyranny in every form, shape, and appearance was their disdain and abhorrence." The Stamp Act seemed to Adams to be the first step of "a direct and formal design . . . to enslave all America . . . by the introduction of the canon and feudal law" which had forced the Americans' ancestors to emigrate from England. To oppose such a move by a few corrupted individuals—the Grenville ministry—Adams urged Americans "to read, think, speak, and write. . . . In a word, let every sluice of knowledge be opened and set a-flowing" against such "encroachments upon liberty" as the Stamp Act.[21]

While the "Dissertation" was appearing anonymously in the *Boston Gazette,* Adams also drafted the "Instructions of the Town of Braintree," which presented what Adams later called a "decided and spirited" defense of the principle that the colonists could not be taxed by Parliament, "because we are not represented in that assembly." Such measures, he wrote, "have a tendency . . . to divest us of our most essential rights and liberties." For not only was the tax burdensome and unconstitutional, it was to be enforced by an unconstitutional extension of the jurisdiction of admiralty courts, in which the judge decided without a jury. "This part of the act," Adams concluded, "will make an essential change in the constitution of juries, and it is directly repugnant" to the Magna Charta. Indeed, the act would make Americans second-class citizens, for it "will 'make . . . a distinction, and create . . . a difference between the subjects in Great Britain and those in America."[22]

In December, John Adams could look back upon 1765 as "the most remarkable Year of my Life," even though the Stamp Act caused him economic hardship. But constitutional principle was more important than economic interest. The American colonists—"from Georgia to New Hampshire inclusively," he wrote—had stood up against "that enormous Engine, fabricated by the british Parliament, for battering down all the Rights and Liberties of America, I mean the Stamp Act." Adams was pleased that he had been a leader in developing a spirit which had "spread, through the whole Continent. . . . Our Presses have groaned, our Pulpits have thundered, our Legislatures have resolved, our Towns have voted, The Crown Officers have every where trembled, and all their little Tools and Creatures, [have] been afraid to Speak and ashamed to be seen."[23]

Colonial opposition, plus a boycott of British goods, forced Parliament to repeal the Stamp Act. But to preserve its claim to absolute power over the colonies, Parliament also passed the Declaratory Act, asserting "full power and authority to make laws and statutes of sufficient force and validity to bind the colonies and people of America, . . . in all cases whatsoever."[24] In 1766 Adams published three letters blasting the idea of absolute Parliamentary power and stressing the rights of Englishmen—particularly trial by jury—as a defense.[25]

By 1768 his reputation and his law business had grown so much that he decided to move from Braintree to Boston. Shortly after his arrival, the Prerogative Party tried to wean him from the Liberty Side and attach him to the King's Men. An old friend, Attorney General Jonathan Sewall, acting on behalf of the royal governor, Francis Bernard, offered him the position of Advocate General in the Admiralty Court, an offer which seemed designed to seduce him from the "liberty" to the "prerogative" side. Was Adams tempted? He certainly was flattered that Governor Bernard and Lieutenant Governor Thomas Hutchinson rated him so highly in terms of "Talents, Integrity, Reputation, and consequence at the Bar." He also noted that "the Office was lucrative in itself, and [would undoubtedly be] a sure introduction to the most profitable Business in the Province, . . . a first Step in the Ladder of Royal Favour and promotion."[26]

But Adams, who found Parliamentary taxation "wholly inconsistent with all my Ideas of Right, Justice, and Policy," quickly refused the post which would place his duty and his inclinations "so much at Variance."[27] Although Adams made the decision promptly, he did not do so without his usual self-examination. "What," he asked himself, "is the End and Purpose of my Studies, Journeys, Labours . . . ? Am I grasping at Money, or Scheming for Power? Am I planning the Illustration of my Family or the Welfare of my Country? . . . I am mostly intent at present," he answered, "upon collecting a Library, and I find, that a great deal of Thought, and Care, as well as Money, are necessary to assemble an ample and well chosen Assortment of Books. But, when this is done, it is only a means, an Instrument. . . . Fame, Fortune, Power say some, are the Ends intended by a Library. The Service of God, Country, Clients, Fellow Men, say others. Which of these lie nearest my heart?"[28] It was a recurrent question for the young lawyer as it had been for the young student.

Adams's move to Boston gave him even less tranquillity than usual, for the Townshend Acts of 1767 raised once again the question of Parliamentary taxation, along with several new issues: 1) the establishment of a Board of Customs Commissioners in Boston, 2) the stationing of British troops to protect them from the Bostonians, and 3) the use of the revenue to pay the royal governors and judges, thus making them independent of colonial assemblies. When the Massachusetts assembly issued a circular letter protesting the Townshend Acts, the governor dissolved it for refusing to rescind the letter.

Once again Adams took the "liberty" side against the "prerogative" party of the royal governor. Although he handled his growing legal work as usual, his most important cases from 1768 to 1776 were related to the political disputes between Britain and America. Three were spectacularly successful: 1) his defense of John Hancock in 1768–69 against a charge of smuggling in violation of the customs laws, 2) his defense of Michael Corbet and three other sailors in 1769 for killing a lieutenant of the British navy, and 3) his defense of Captain Thomas Preston of the British army for his role in the Boston Massacre. The Hancock case was a protracted admiralty case that pitted Adams against his friend, Advocate General Jonathan Sewall. Following the line of reasoning he had laid out in his "Dissertation on the Feudal Law," Adams challenged the constitutionality of legislation that denied his client a jury trial. It repealed "Magna Charta as far as America is concerned," he argued, and degraded Hancock "below the Rank of an Englishman."[29] Moreover, Adams argued that the statute had been "made without our consent. My client, Mr. Hancock, never consented to it; he never voted for it himself, and he never voted for any man to make such a law for him." After a trial of five months—it was "a painfull Drudgery I had of his cause," John Adams later wrote[30]—his defense was successful, "one of his major accomplishments as a lawyer," according to Lyman Butterfield.[31]

The Corbet case was also argued in Admiralty Court, and Adams later regretted not writing up his arguments in pamphlet form in order to "possibly procure for us for the future the Benefit of Juries in such Cases."[32] Corbet and his companions were crew members of a Marblehead, Massachusetts, packet, who resisted impressment by the British navy off Marblehead. When Lieutenant Henry G. Panton and an armed press gang from the British frigate *Rose* disregarded warnings not to come aboard the packet, Corbet threw a harpoon that cut Panton's jugular vein, killing him instantly. When Adams discovered a statute passed in Queen Anne's reign which prohibited impressments in America, the court ruled that the Massachusetts sailors had killed the lieutenant in self-defense and issued a decree of justifiable homicide. Thus Adams converted a murder trial into a legal forum to discuss two fundamental issues of political and constitutional significance: the right to jury trials, and the right of the Royal Navy to impress American seamen.

Adams's defense of Captain Preston, commander of the British troops in the Boston Massacre, was even more sensational. The opposition of Bostonians to the Townshend duties had led to the stationing of two regiments in Boston to protect the customs commissioners in 1768. "My daily Reflections for two years, at the Sight of those Soldiers before my door"—their "Spirit Stirring Drum and . . . Earpiercing fife aroused me and my family early enough every morning," Adams wrote in his *Autobiography*—"was a strong proof to me that the determination in Great Britain to subjugate Us, was too deep and inveterate ever to be altered by Us."[33]

The natural antagonism between citizens and redcoats led to the snowballing of the troops that degenerated into a mob attack, an order to fire, and the death of five Bostonians. The morning after the Boston Massacre, Captain Preston asked John Adams to defend him against charges of murder. Convinced that "this would be as important a Cause as ever was tryed in any Court or Country of the World" and that lawyers ought "to be independent and impartial at all Times And in every Circumstance," Adams accepted, even though it meant "hazarding a Popularity very general and very hardly earned."[34]

The trial of Preston and the British soldiers resulted in acquittal, and Adams later reflected that his defense "was one of the most gallant, generous, manly and disinterested Actions of my whole Life, and one of the best Pieces of Service I ever rendered my Country."[35] Looking back in 1805 he wrote: "Although the Clamour was very loud, among some Sorts of People, it has been a great Consolation to me through Life, that I acted in this Business with steady impartiality, and conducted it to so happy an Issue."[36] Despite the clamor, Adams did not lose his popularity with the populace, for in the midst of the proceedings in 1770, he was elected to the Massachusetts assembly as a representative of Boston by 418 out of 536 votes cast.

On the day of the Boston Massacre, the British government repealed all of the Townshend duties except that on tea. That was retained as an assertion of Parliamentary authority, for as George Grenville had argued, "a pepper-corn in acknowledgement of a right is of more value than millions without it."[37]

Mentally and physically exhausted, Adams decided in April 1771 to drop out of public life. Moving his family back to "still, calm, happy Braintree," he resolved to devote himself to law and farming. "Farewell Politicks," he told his diary.[38] For almost a year and a half, he kept his resolution as best he could, working at his law practice, doing some farming, and attempting to regain his health through physical activity and visits to mineral springs in Connecticut. By November 1772, however, the demands of his law practice forced him to move back to Boston.

At peace with his decision to "avoid Politicks, Political Clubbs, Town Meetings, General Court, &c. &c. &c.,"[39] John Adams could confide to his diary in January 1773, that "I never was happier, in my whole life, than I have been since I returned to Boston."[40] Yet within three months he was once again deeply involved in political controversy. From then on he entered into the political battles of Massachusetts, the United Colonies, and the United States without looking back.

The events which precipitated Adams's reentry into the political arena in that three-month period were threefold. The first was a speech by Governor Thomas Hutchinson on January 6, 1773, to the General Court in which he claimed that Parliament's authority over the colonies was supreme; according to Adams, that claim raised "the greatest Question ever yet agitated."[41] "I know of no line," the governor told the Massachusetts legislators "that can be drawn between the supreme authority of Parliament and the total independence of the colonies. It is impossible [that] there should be two independent legislatures in one and the same state, for . . . two legislative bodies will make two governments as distinct as the Kingdoms of England and Scotland before the Union" in 1707.[42]

The Massachusetts assembly promptly dissented. "If there be no such line," Adams wrote in the legislature's reply, "the consequence is either that the colonies are the vassals of the Parliament or that they are totally independent" of Parliament. Conceding that "it is difficult, . . . to draw a line of distinction between the universal authority of Parliament over the colonies and no authority at all," Adams and the legislators made it clear that they would never agree to "be reduced to a state of vassalage," subject to an "absolute uncontrolled supreme power." By accepting the governor's terms of argument, Adams and the Massachusetts legislature articulated a new theory that Parliament, instead of having power to bind the colonies in all cases whatsoever, had no authority in the colonies whatsoever. They did not argue that they were independent of Great Britain, however, for they pointed out that as long as they were "united in one head and common Sovereign [the king]" and did not interfere with each other, they could "live happily in that connection and mutually support and protect each other."[43]

Next Adams published a series of letters in the *Boston Gazette* attacking a proposal which would have made colonial judges of the Superior Court responsible only to the Crown, forbidding them "to receive their salaries as usual from the Grants of the House of Representatives." According to Adams, this would make the judges "entirely dependent on the Crown for Bread [as] well as office."[44] Finally, in late March 1773, he received a packet of "purloined letters " from Benjamin Franklin in England, letters written in 1768–69 by Governor Hutchinson and others. In one, Hutchinson concluded that "there must be an Abridgment of what are called English Liberties" in America. "I doubt whether it is possible [that] . . . a Colony . . . shall enjoy all the Liberty of the Parent State."[45] This letter and the others seemed to Adams to show the "secret, dark, and deep" purposes of Hutchinson to undermine American liberties and "ruin this Country."[46]

Finally, Adams's full re-initiation into politics came in May 1773 when he was again elected to the Massachusetts legislature. His immediate reaction was to examine his heart and soul: "What will be expected of me? What Duties and Obligations will result to me, from an Election? What duties to my God, my King, my Country, My Family, my Friends, myself? . . . What Self denials and mortifications shall I be obliged to bear?" And his immediate response was predictable. Although his assignment might be "arduous and disagreeable," he would act "a fearless, intrepid, undaunted Part, at all Hazards—tho," he added after some deliberation, "it shall be my Endeavour likewise to act a prudent, cautious and considerate Part."[47]

In the Tea Party crisis that brought the controversy with Britain to a climax, Adams did indeed play "a fearless, intrepid, and undaunted Part." He rejoiced at the dumping of illegally taxed tea into Boston Harbor, calling it "the grandest Event, which has ever yet happened since the Controversy with Britain opened!" "To let it be landed," he wrote, "would be giving up the Principle of Taxation by Parliamentary Authority, against which the Continent have struggled for 10 years, it was loosing all our labour for 10 years and subjecting ourselves and our Posterity forever to Egyptian Taskmasters—to Burthens, Indignities, to Ignominy, Reproach and Contempt, to Desolation and Oppression, to Poverty and Servitude." Landing the tea and paying the tax, he felt, would have constituted "the final Ruin of our Constitution of Government, and of all American Liberties." Dumping the tea meant that the public had crossed "the river and cut away the bridge."[48]

Soon thereafter, he attempted to counter what seemed to him to be yet another threat to these liberties, the payment of Superior Court judges' salaries by the Crown, by instigating impeachment proceedings against justices who accepted such salaries. He then helped draw up the legal articles of impeachment which, although rejected by the governor's council, had a wide impact on the public because of their circulation in the press. By September 1774 the proceedings of the Superior Court had come to a standstill as patriotic jurors refused one by one to serve in a court whose justices stood impeached. As Adams noted in his *Autobiography*, "the Court never sat again until a new one was appointed by the [Patriot] Council . . . after the Battle of Lexington on the 19th of April 1775."[49]

Throughout the spring and early summer of 1774, as the contest between the colonies and Parliament intensified, John Adams was on the front lines in Massachusetts. It would be erroneous, however, to portray Adams as pushing the colonies toward the independence they later declared. Rather, he viewed the contest in a constitutional light. As British citizens, the Americans had certain rights under the British constitution which, in Adams's view, Parliament was attempting to usurp. His purpose—in refuting Hutchinson in January 1773, in opposing Crown salaries for judges, in applauding the dumping of tea in Boston Harbor—was to redress the constitutional balance and to restore to the colonies and the colonists their legal rights. In April 1774, for example, Adams wrote confidently to his friend James Warren that neither side felt disposed to "bring the question to a complete decision." Instead, he suggested, "we shall oscillate like a pendulum, . . . for many years to come, and never obtain a complete redress of American grievances, nor submit to an absolute establishment of parliamentary authority, but be trimming between both, as we have been for ten years past, for more years to come than you and I shall live."[50]

But the time for trimming was past. Instead of repealing the tea tax, Parliament, which had repealed both the Stamp and the Townshend Acts, passed a series of Coercive Acts designed to punish and isolate Massachusetts for the Boston Tea Party. These acts closed the port of Boston until the tea was paid for, radically altered the Massachusetts chartered form of government by transferring from the assembly to the king the power to choose the governor's council, placed a ban on town meetings, provided for the transportation of specified offenders to England for trial, and for the first time since the Boston Massacre quartered troops in the town of Boston. At the same time General Thomas Gage, the commander-in-chief of British troops in North America, succeeded the civilian Hutchinson as governor.

With Boston virtually occupied, the other colonies sprang to the support of Massachusetts. To meet this sweeping assertion of Parliamentary supremacy, which went far beyond the mere matter of taxation, the Virginia House of Burgesses issued a call for a congress of all the American colonies. Like the Stamp Act Congress, the Continental Congress was designed "to consult upon the present State of the Colonies" and to organize a united resistance to further encroachments upon the rights to which Americans believed they were entitled.[51]

On June 17, 1774, the Massachusetts General Court cleared its galleries, locked its doors, and appointed a committee to represent the province at the Continental Congress. John Adams was one of the five delegates chosen. Characteristically, he reacted to the "grand Scene open before me," with both exultation and trepidation. Flattered to be chosen to attend "an assembly of the wisest Men upon the Continent," he experienced "unutterable Anxiety" at the prospect. "I feel my self unequal to this Business," he scribbled in his diary. He added:

I muse, I mope, I ruminate.—I am often In Reveries and Brown Studies.—The Objects before me, are too grand, and multifarious for my Comprehension. . . . We are deficient in Genius, in Education, in Travel, in Fortune—in every Thing. . . . God Grant us Wisdom, and Fortitude! Should the Opposition be suppressed, should this Country submit, what Infamy and Ruin! God forbid. Death in any Form is less terrible.[52]

On August 10 the Massachusetts delegation left from Boston "amidst the kind wishes and fervent prayers of every man . . . for our health and success."[53] Passing through Connecticut, New York, and New Jersey, they were met at almost every town along the way by delegations of patriots. In every colony, he wrote Abigail, "we have been treated with unbounded civility, complaisance, and respect."[54]

On September 5, the delegates gathered at City Tavern in Philadelphia and walked together to Carpenters Hall. As Adams had predicted, the Congress consisted of a distinguished group of colonial leaders broadly representative of the provincial conventions that had chosen and instructed them. An extralegal body, the Continental Congress included delegates from every colony except Georgia. The fifty-five representatives were headed by the Massachusetts and Virginia delegates—radicals like John and Sam Adams, Patrick Henry, and Richard Henry Lee, moderates like George Washington and Peyton Randolph. The only conservative contingents came from New York and Pennsylvania—men like Joseph Galloway, John Jay, and James Duane.

Adams was especially impressed by the Virginians, who appeared to "be the most spirited and consistent, of any. [Benjamin] Harrison said he would have come on foot rather than not come. [Richard] Bland said he would have gone, upon this Occasion, if it had been to Jericho."[55] In all, he wrote Abigail, "there is in the Congress a collection of the greatest men upon this continent in point of abilities, virtues, and fortunes."[56]

As a member of a committee to prepare a declaration of the rights of the colonists, John Adams served as penman of the Congress, drafting the crucial resolution dealing with Parlia-

mentary authority over the colonies. When the whole committee came to that question—"the Essence of the whole Controversy," according to Adams—it could not agree.[57] Turning
to Adams, John Rutledge of South Carolina asked him to draft
a statement. His resolution denied Parliament any authority
over the colonies except, "from the necessity of the case, . . .
the regulation of our external commerce," but it claimed allegiance to the king.[58] Ultimate authority rested not with Parliament but with the people:

> [T]he foundation of English liberty, and of all free government, is a
> right in the people to participate in their legislative council: and as the
> English colonists are not represented, and from their local and other
> circumstances, cannot properly be represented in the British parlia-
> ment, they are entitled to a free and exclusive power of legislation in
> their several provincial legislatures, where their right of representa-
> tion can alone be preserved, in all cases of taxation and internal polity,
> subject only to the negative of their sovereign, in such manner as has
> been heretofore used and accustomed.[59]

The principle established, Congress then enacted a system
of retaliatory measures against the Coercive Acts. Since commercial boycotts had been instrumental in creating pressure
on Parliament to repeal the Stamp Act and the Townshend
duties, Congress again adopted a series of nonimportation,
nonexportation, and nonconsumption agreements as "the
means most proper to be pursued for a restoration of our
rights."[60] To enforce these retaliatory measures, Congress established "The Association," a system of local and provincial
committees who were to inspect customs entries, confiscate
illegal importations, publish the names of offending merchants, and generally to "encourage frugality, economy, and
industry . . . and will discountenance . . . every species of ex-
travagance and dissipation, especially all horse-racing, and all
kinds of gaming, cock-fighting, exhibition of shews, plays, and
other expensive diversions and entertainments."[61] As a delegate from the colony where those rights were being most
severely tested, John Adams spoke and voted for the strongest
actions possible, including preparation for war—a precau-
tionary measure.

Before the Continental Congress adjourned, it resolved

"that another Congress should be held on the tenth day of May next, unless the redress of grievances, which we have desired, be obtained before that time."[62] Adams doubted that the actions of Congress would dissuade the British. Back in Massachusetts he attended the Provincial Congress as a delegate from Braintree. At the same time he started composing replies to a series of loyalist letters by Daniel Leonard which began appearing in the Boston newspapers in December 1774. Signing himself "Novanglus" (New England), John Adams attempted to counteract Leonard's "Subtlety of Art and Address, wonderfully calculated to keep Up the Spirits of their Party, to depress ours, to spread intimidation and to make Proselytes among those, whose Principles and Judgment give Way to their fears."[63] The Novanglus essays appeared in weekly installments in the *Boston Gazette* from January 1775 until April 19, when the Battle of Lexington, as Adams wrote, "changed the Instruments of Warfare from the Penn to the Sword."[64] Skillfully employing historical argument, Novanglus demonstrated that it was "the wicked policy of the tories . . . to break down the fences of a free constitution, and deprive the people at large of all share in the government." Rejecting Leonard's claim that the patriots actually sought independence, Adams asserted that "the Whigs acknowledge a subordination to the king . . . [and] to Parliament, as far as regulation of trade."[65]

The members of the Second Continental Congress convened in Philadelphia on May 10, 1775, while the colonies were still reverberating with the news of Lexington and Concord and "the shot heard round the world." Although no war had been declared, blood had been shed, and a virtual state of war existed between the colonists and soldiers in Massachusetts. The Provincial Assembly of that colony had sent a written request to the Continental Congress for the creation of a Continental army. As a delegate from the beleaguered colony, John Adams not only backed that move but also wanted Congress to authorize Massachusetts and other colonies to call conventions "to institute Governments for themselves, under their own Authority."[66] Congress was not yet ready to support this radical proposal for such governments, but it did proceed with the selection of a commander-in-chief for the army at Boston. At John Adams's suggestion, "the modest and virtuous, the amiable, generous and brave George Washington" was appointed "to command all the Continental forces raised or to be raised for the defense of American liberty." "This appointment will have a great effect," thought Adams, "in cementing and securing the union of these colonies." He urged his fellow New Englanders to welcome the Virginian "with all that confidence and affection, that politeness and respect, which is due to one of the most important characters in the world. The liberties of America," he concluded without exaggeration, "depend upon him, in a great degree."[67]

The delegates to Congress adopted a vigorous Declaration of the Causes and Necessity of Taking up Arms, the joint product of the radical, young Thomas Jefferson, and the conservative, old John Dickinson:

[T]he arms we have been compelled by our enemies to assume, we will, . . . employ for the preservation of our liberties; being with one mind resolved to die freemen rather than live slaves. . . . [W]e mean not to dissolve that union which has so long and so happily subsisted between us. . . . We have not raised armies with ambitious designs of separating from Great Britain, and establishing independent States.[68]

But John Adams was not so sure about the desirability of union with Britain after news of Bunker Hill arrived in Philadelphia on the day that General Washington left for Boston. He soon grew impatient with the interminable wranglings and indecision of Congress, complaining to Abigail of "the Fidgets, the Whims, the Caprice, the Vanity, the Superstition, the irritability" of his fellow delegates.[69] He was especially critical of John Dickinson's conciliatory "Olive Branch" petition to the king, which he later called "this Measure of imbecility."[70] In July he wrote a critical letter to his friend James Warren, reporting that John Dickinson, "a certain great Fortune and piddling Genius, whose fame had been trumpeted so loudly, has given a silly Cast to our whole Doings." "We are," he added, "between Hawk and Buzzard," when "we ought to have had in our Hands a month ago the whole Legislative, executive and judicial [powers] of the whole Continent."[71]

This letter, which reflected Adams's exasperation with the conciliationists, was intercepted by the British and created a sensation when General Gage published it in a Massachusetts newspaper. Adams's open avowal of independence and his criticism of Dickinson would, so the British thought, produce further quarrels among the members of Congress and a division of the colonies. Adams had few regrets about the letter's publication, however, feeling, as he wrote to Abigail, that rather than having "bad Effects, as the Tories intended," it brought "fresh Proofs that every Body is coming fast into every political Sentiment contained in them."[72]

Notwithstanding Adams's complaints about the equivocation of the Second Continental Congress, it accomplished much more than the previous one. Though it stopped short of independence, it emphasized a vigorous defense of colonial rights, establishing an army with Washington at its head, issuing the first Continental money, founding a postal system, and beginning the consideration of a confederation of the colonies. Recessing for the month of August, the Congress agreed to meet again in September 1775.

When Congress reconvened, the chief issues included supplying the new Continental army, establishing a trade policy for the colonies, and creating a navy. For three months, Adams worked from seven in the morning until late at night serving committees and attending debates in Congress. As a member of a committee to advise the colonies on their internal government during "the present dispute" with Britain, he helped draft a resolution directing them to assume certain self-governing powers for the duration, thus encouraging a state of semi-independence. When he learned that the king had rejected Dickinson's "Olive Branch" petition and that Parliament had retaliated by prohibiting all trade and intercourse with the rebellious colonies, Adams was exultant:

I know not whether you [Horatio Gates] have seen the Act of Parliament call'd the restraining Act or prohibitory Act, or Piratical Act or Plundering Act or Act of Independency, for by all these Titles it is called. I think the most apposite is the Act of Independency, for King, Lords and Commons have united in Sundering this Country and that I think forever. It is a compleate Dismemberment of the British

Empire. It throws thirteen Colonies out of the Royal Protection, and levels all Distinctions and makes us independent in spight of supplications and Entreaties.[73]

In February 1776 he obtained a copy of Thomas Paine's *Common Sense* which, he thought, contained "a great deal of good sense" on the subject of independence. Although Adams agreed with Paine's common sense on independence, he was highly critical of his recommendations for state government. The pamphlet's author, he was convinced, had "very inadequate ideas of what is proper and necessary to be done, in order to form constitutions for single colonies, as well as a great model of union for the whole."[74] Hoping to counteract Paine's ideas on constitutional construction and realizing that, as independence became increasingly likely, the colonies would need a model on which to frame their governments, Adams drew up a document setting forth his ideas on government. The essay was published in April 1776 under the title *Thoughts on Government.*

Convinced that "the happiness of society is the end of government," Adams wrote that "the blessings of society depend entirely on the constitutions of government." Continuing, he asked, "When, before the present epocha, had three millions of people full power and a fair opportunity to form and establish the wisest and happiest government that human wisdom can contrive?" That government, Adams was convinced, should not be a unicameral system, as suggested in Paine's *Common Sense.* Instead, it should be a carefully balanced bicameral system. The first branch, elected by the people, should choose the second, and the two together should choose a governor. The judiciary branch should be distinct from the legislative and executive, and independent of both, so that "it may be a check upon both, as both should be checks" upon it.[75]

John Adams was instrumental in prodding Congress toward independence between April and July 1776. The first step came May 10 when Congress adopted his resolution instructing each colony to establish such government "as shall . . . best conduce to the Happiness and Safety of their Constituents in particular, and America in general."[76] Adams wrote the preamble, which was, as he told Abigail, "a total absolute independence, not only of her [Britain's] Parliament, but of . . . [the] Crown."[77] By May 20, 1776, he was exultant, reporting that "Every Post and every Day rolls in upon Us Independence like a Torrent."[78]

With the colonies establishing constitutions and transforming themselves into independent states, the stage was set for the final break by Congress. On June 7, Richard Henry Lee introduced resolutions urging 1) independence, stating "that the colonies are, and of right ought to be, free and independent States," 2) a plan of confederation to create a union of the colonies, and 3) a system of foreign alliances to obtain foreign aid.[79] Adams served on all three committees created to accomplish these ends. Jefferson asked him to draft the Declaration of Independence, but Adams thought that Massachusetts should not hog the spotlight. Instead, he urged Jefferson the Virginian to take the lead, just as he had asked Washington, a Virginian, to take military command. He told Jefferson that "you are a Virginian, and a Virginian ought to appear at the head of this business. . . . I am obnoxious, suspected, and unpopular. You are very much otherwise. . . . [And finally,] you can write ten times better than I can."[80]

But Jefferson was no debater and it was Adams who defended the committee Resolution for Independence. When Congress adopted the Resolution on July 2, Richard Stockton, a New Jersey delegate, called John Adams "the Atlas of American Independence," and Jefferson later wrote that Adams was "the pillar of it's support on the floor of Congress, it's ablest advocate and defender against the multifarious assaults it encountered."[81]

On that day, July 2, 1776, Adams's fame was fixed. Had he dropped dead on July 3 he would have died a great man. He went on, of course, to a distinguished career as a diplomat, helping to negotiate the peace treaty that ended the War for Independence and confirmed the creation of a new nation. He also wrote the Massachusetts Constitution of 1780. And he was, of course, Washington's successor as president of the United States, living on after retirement in 1801 for a quarter of a century to see his son, John Quincy Adams, become president. Never popular—he was defeated in his bid for reelection as president—he left office after negotiating a satisfactory conclusion to the Quasi War with France, a move that won him the enmity of the hawkish wing of the Federalist Party headed by Alexander Hamilton. But he put peace above party and was so pleased with his diplomatic triumph that he proposed that his epitaph should read: "Here lies John Adams, who took upon himself the responsibility of peace with France in the year 1800." Vain for fame, Adams sought not momentary popularity but lasting approbation.

And finally, nearly 150 years after his death on July 4, 1826—he and Jefferson died on that fiftieth anniversary of the Declaration of Independence—John Adams is at long last receiving the belated approbation he so earnestly sought throughout his lifetime. For at no time in the past has he ever stood higher in the public estimation than he does today. He was the leading character in the recent motion picture, *1776,* and before that in the musical play which ran on Broadway for years. His correspondence with Thomas Jefferson has been published in two volumes by Lester Cappon,[82] and his most thorough biography, based upon the microfilm edition of all the Adams Family Papers, has been written in two volumes by Page Smith.[83] And recently *Newsweek* published a two-volume biography of John Adams in his own words in its series on The Founding Fathers.[84]

But the most enduring monument to John Adams in the twentieth century will be the multivolume edition of The Adams Papers being edited by Lyman H. Butterfield and others. Already thirteen volumes are in print—five volumes of his diary and autobiography, three volumes of his legal papers, four volumes of family correspondence, and one volume of portraits, with dozens more yet to come.[85] Butterfield, who has analyzed Adams's writings for the past twenty years, argues that Adams "emerges not only as one of the indispensable guides to what happened during the birth and early years of the United States of America, but also as one of the most valuable guides to understanding humanity with all its strengths and frailties."[86]

Perhaps the most fitting measure of the man, however, was

made by John F. Kennedy, who took time out while president of the United States to review Adams's *Diary and Autobiography* for the *American Historical Review*. According to Kennedy, John Adams "bequeathed to us two extraordinary and important qualities: conscience, Puritan conscience, and courage—the courage of those who look to other days and other times." And later President Kennedy added other elements to his appraisal of Adams: "honesty, tenacity, and pungent good sense," plus "the honest directness of his reactions." His "constant self-analysis[,] combined with an underlying self-esteem[,] was not debilitating but a prod to fresh achievement. This ability to blend private life and public activity, reflection and practical action, conscience and courage was for Adams a liberating force."[87]

And then, looking down the hall of history from Adams's time to our own, Mr. Kennedy on that bright October day after eight months in office as president of the United States, paid tribute not only to John Adams but to the present generation. "I congratulate this country," he said; "I congratulate us all—in being part of the legacy which President John Adams left to us."[88]

6

JAMES IREDELL AND THE ORIGINS OF AMERICAN FEDERALISM

In discussing the American Revolution and the origins of American federalism, my intention is to approach the subject through the ideas and experiences of one man, James Iredell, about whom most Americans know little if anything. "Parson" Weems, Washington's biographer and author of the cherry tree story, said that the great men of the Revolution went to heaven with pomp and ceremony. By that standard, if not others, Washington must have been the greatest, for Weems gives us a rarity: an account of Washington's going.

Swift on angels' wings the brightening saint ascended; while voices more than human were heard warbling through the happy regions, and hymning the great procession towards the gates of heaven. His glorious coming was seen far off; and myriads of mighty angels hastened forth, with golden harps, to welcome the honoured stranger.[1]

Unfortunately, I cannot say whether James Iredell ever went to heaven, or if so, in what circumstances. He confessed to his diary that he occasionally drank too much wine, and he also conceded as a young man that his thoughts about the fairer sex were not wholly of the kind to divulge publicly. But all of this is not very relevant, especially since Iredell is traditionally pictured as a secondary figure in American history, and perhaps rightly so. For this quiet, retiring, unassuming North Carolinian was never center stage in the arena of public affairs. He never held elective office, never served in Washington's Continental army (he hired a substitute). Nor has he received a scholarly biography. Indeed the one biography of

Iredell appeared in the 1850s and is largely a collection of his letters. The author, Griffith McRee, was a member of the Iredell family, who eschewed textual fidelity and rarely breached the canons of Victorian taste (despite a promise to reveal warts and all), who sought to immortalize Iredell in printer's type, and who wrote as a Southern literary nationalist, determined to show Northern historians in the Age of James Buchanan a thing or two—with their "Yankee cunning" they had been out to disparage the history of the South in general and the history of North Carolina in particular.[2]

Above all, Iredell was a thinker and a writer, an intellectual by any definition of that inexact word. His life was a life of the mind. And yet in the eighteenth century—in America, at least—one had small opportunity for a cloistered existence; there was no research professorship, no think-tank slot with a private foundation or institute. Trained in the law in the fashion of his day—by reading under the direction of a senior attorney—he became a practicing lawyer, state judge, state attorney general, and eventually a justice of the United States Supreme Court.

But we are getting ahead of our story. We must begin with Iredell, a British customs official at Edenton, North Carolina, in the late 1760s and early 1770s. Now it would certainly seem strange that a Crown servant would be able to make a contribution to American federalism. For we know what happened when the time came for men to choose between independence and loyalty to the Mother Country in 1776: almost without exception royal officeholders opted for George III. Indeed, the customs men throughout the dozen or so years of turmoil after 1763 were zealous in upholding the laws of Parliament.

Like most royal servants, Iredell was a native Englishman, whose widowed mother and several younger brothers lived in Bristol and depended upon him for considerable financial support. The combined influence of highly placed relatives of the McCartney-McCulloh clan, had brought seventeen-year-old James to Edenton in 1768, first to serve as comptroller of customs and then, in 1774, to occupy the more lucrative collectorship itself. Still other advantages and opportunities might one day come to such a well-entrenched Crown employee, perhaps even elevation to the royal council.

But if Iredell had close ties with his homeland, he had also developed a strong attachment to North Carolina, particularly the Johnston family of Edenton. Samuel Johnston was a highly respected lawyer and an influential assemblyman, a nephew of an earlier royal governor and owner of the largest library in the province (it still exists today at Hayes plantation).[3] Johnston agreed that Iredell in his spare time could study law with him, and there developed an exceedingly close relationship between them, undoubtedly strengthened by Iredell's marriage to Johnston's sister Hannah. Iredell learned, by observation and by reading, of the law and its workings. Just as the two men discussed the famous writings of the great legal scholars such as Bacon, Coke, and Blackstone, so too they discussed an immediate legal matter of concern to most Americans: the encroachments of the British Parliament upon colonial liberties.

Johnston explained in detail to Iredell the colonists' position on taxation and other things that had generated controversy with the Mother Country. Johnston himself was in the forefront of the movement for American rights, later serving as presiding officer at two provincial congresses. Although Iredell became convinced that Parliament had passed numerous acts harmful to the provincials and in violation of their constitutional rights, he nonetheless loved England and the British Empire, and he recognized that he would lose much in terms of family and economic rewards if America declared her independence and if he chose to cast his lot with the new nation. For Iredell the burdensome problem was this: how could American liberties be restored and guaranteed without separating from the empire? In a series of four essays penned between 1773 and 1776, Iredell sought a solution.[4] In doing so, he turned his attention for the first time to what we have come to call federalism.

By federalism, of course, we mean a system of political order where governmental powers are separated and distributed among different governments, each with its own authority and sphere of operation. The British Empire before 1763, for all practical purposes, had functioned as a federal system. While king and Parliament had concerned themselves with the regulation of commerce and other external matters, the colonies had been almost entirely left alone in the management of their own internal affairs. Historians have sometimes described the colonial legislatures as little parliaments, and with good reason since these local bodies grew impressively in power and influence in the first six decades of the eighteenth century.[5]

Those changes had never been encouraged, much less understood, by British politicians and administrators. They had, in truth, altered the nature of the empire and the constitution—a constitution, it will be recalled, that was unwritten, that derived much of its meaning from precedent and tradition. And assuredly precedent and tradition had wrought profound mutations in the workings of the empire in the 150 years since the planting of the first permanent English settlements in the New World.

Englishmen failed to see what American writers, soon joined by James Iredell, were in essence advocating: namely, to freeze into legal shape the practical working empire of 1763. To Iredell, it appeared that people in the Mother Country had generated a senseless forest of controversy as to American motives. Any wish for independence had never been an ingredient in the broth of conflict. "Base and wicked assertion to the contrary," he was convinced that "an honorable reconciliation" stood as the "most earnest object of every Man's wish and attention." No one mentioned the idea of independence except with "horror and indignation."

Before 1763, asserted Iredell, Americans generally were satisfied with the imperial relationship between the English-speaking peoples on both sides of the Atlantic. The Acts of Trade and Navigation, which had regulated the external commerce of the empire for a century, had been "mutually beneficial." While several provisions might be deemed "hard and rigorous," the restrictions upon colonial intercourse were nevertheless "a natural and just compensation" for the manifold blessing that flowed from affiliation with the "great and powerful" British nation.

The ultimate victory over the Bourbon monarchies in the Seven Years' War should have led to an even closer bond between the various spokes in the wheel of empire. But that did not occur, explained Iredell, because England tried to change the nature of the imperial relationship, to dominate it to the point that America's wealth was to be wholly for the benefit of Britain. "The pretence" in 1765 for the Stamp Act, "the first great encroachment[,] was to provide for our defence." But in the postwar years, with Canada in British hands and France no longer an immediate threat, the need for stationing regulars in America was nonexistent.

Iredell's political tracts make abundantly clear his interpretation of the origins of the Revolution. The colonists were defending constitutional principles, particularly the right of no taxation without representation. The very Britishness of the Americans made them stand up for their beliefs. They contend "for an exclusive right of the disposal of . . . [their] own property," which was "one of the most essential privileges of the British Constitution, and that which is the principal guard and protection of all others."

To set forth the constitutional limits to Parliamentary power was a demanding intellectual challenge for America's finest minds, and, fortunately for America, most of those minds were in the legal profession. Small wonder that the American Revolution has been called a lawyers' revolution, especially when we recall that men such as Iredell, James Otis, John Dickinson, John Adams, Thomas Jefferson, and James Wilson plied the attorney's trade. Or when we remember the warning of Edmund Burke to Parliament in 1775: "In no country perhaps in the world is the law so general a study" as in America. "The profession itself is numerous and powerful, and in most provinces it takes the lead. . . . This study renders men acute, inquisitive, dexterous, prompt in attack, ready in defence, [and] full of resources. . . . They augur misgovernment at a distance; and sniff the approach of tyranny in every tainted breeze."[6]

When Americans had initially sought to constrict Parliament's jurisdiction during the Stamp Act crisis, they had experienced an almost completely negative reaction in Britain, where it was trumpeted that the taxing power formed an

essential part of every supreme legislative authority. Iredell
believed the colonists had not put forth their most effective
case in voicing their objections to the constitutionality of Parliamentary taxation at the time of the Stamp Act. They had
weakened their argument by making a distinction between
"internal and external taxation," although their distinction
stemmed mainly from carelessness and not from intellectual
conviction. In the past the word *taxes* had sometimes been
loosely employed to refer to payments that were made under
the old Acts of Trade and Navigation. But they were "more
properly (when the subject was critically examined) called
duties" and had "reference to commercial purposes." Taxes,
on the other hand, "are the proper name for impositions,
where money alone is the object." In short, when some Americans apparently deferred to Parliament's levying external
taxes, they actually did not mean taxes, but only the small,
incidental sums that had accrued to the Mother Country in the
course of regulating imperial trade for the well-being of both
England and America. Perhaps the confusion was not only
excusable but even logical. After all, we have stressed that the
colonists saw the empire in terms of internal and external
spheres, of distributed political authority, or federalism.

American confusion gave Parliament an excuse to saddle
America with external taxes, the so-called Townshend Duties
in 1767, on lead, tea, paint, paper, and glass. Now Americans
spelled out what they had previously neglected to clarify, asserted Iredell. For the Townshend measures were "in principle, in substance, and nearly in danger . . . the same as the one
we had been cursed with" earlier. Although in 1770 Parliament withdrew all the Townshend taxes save the one on tea,
that remaining tax "afterwards proved a fruitful source" of
contention. Parliament, in seeking to aid the financially dis-
tressed East India Company, pushed the consumption of the
dutied brew in America in the Tea Act of 1773. That in turn
produced a stiffening of colonial backs, culminating in the
Boston Tea Party.

Iredell proudly stated that the Americans did not submit,
nor did they subsequently sit idly by when Parliament responded to the Boston Tea Party by passing the Coercive Acts,

or Intolerable Acts, which were aimed at Massachusetts. "What was the case of Massachusetts Bay," predicted Iredell, "might be that of New York, Pennsylvania, and any of the others tomorrow. . . . Were they to stand *single,* each might be made an immediate and disgraceful prey to an unmerciful and cruel Tyranny."

Not only had Parliament rejected the colonists' position that they could only be taxed by their own legislatures, but that body had, in the Coercive Acts, hatched severely repressive measures that obviously had no bearing on taxation. Could the colonists still safely maintain that while Parliament had no taxing powers whatever over America, it possessed regulatory authority over commerce and other connections of empire? Already the colonists, for the most part unconsciously, had adopted a concept of sovereignty at odds with the long-prevailing view. The empire was not a unitary structure in which one political organ exercised total sovereignty, for the colonial assemblies were, in effect, absolute in their own internal domains.

To defend themselves against the Coercive Acts and any future vindictive laws that might fall under the general regulatory power that they had previously acknowledged, the colonists were compelled to find new weapons in their intellectual arsenal, which would also prohibit the supremacy of Parliament in the external sphere. Since Parliament, in Iredell's opinion, would not agree to recognize boundaries to its jurisdiction, and since it rejected a federal conception of the empire, the Americans would have to deny that body any binding authority in order to guarantee that the colonies could remain in the empire with their freedoms intact. Parliament had driven the colonists into an all or nothing position. Or as Burke put it, when you push him severely, the boar will turn upon the hunter. If sovereignty and liberty cannot be reconciled, it is obvious which men will choose.

Could this all or nothing stance have been avoided? Possibly so, since Americans gradually came to perceive the constitution of Britain as primarily principles rather than institutions. Somehow a way was needed to make Englishmen see that Parliament itself was not a part of the constitution, and therefore its acts must be in conformity with fundamental or supreme law, terms which, in American political literature, became increasingly used as synonymous with constitutionalism.[7] Was there no agency or tribunal that might declare when Parliament had overstepped itself, when it had violated the constitution? To be sure, there had operated a check on colonial laws; the Privy Council's oversight regarding provincial legislation constituted a kind of judicial review. Had one existed for Parliament, the empire might have been preserved, the colonial conception of federalism might have prevailed.

One of the first Americans to gingerly feel his way into this murky area was James Otis, who in the 1761 Writs of Assistance Case had announced that it was the obligation of the courts to expose the illegality of an act of Parliament in conflict with the constitution. Three years later in his *Rights of the British Colonies* he repeated the same argument in more detail. But while Otis maintained that the courts might chart instances of Parliament's transgressions, it would then be up to Parliament itself to repeal its own acts. Here was a fatal flaw in Otis's analysis of how American redress might be obtained. In fact, despite his somewhat advanced thinking for his time, he was soon to fall behind other American writers, especially on one crucial point: he continued to believe that Parliament was itself part of the constitution.[8] Thus, the courts could only urge, not compel, Parliament to reverse itself. Of course, we know that the British courts never responded as Otis had indicated they should; nor is it likely that, if they had, Parliament would have withdrawn any of its acts.

In time Iredell would develop more fully the idea of judicial review, minus the limitations of Otis's approach. Iredell himself does not appear to have used that argument at this time, although, given later remarks, he probably began to contemplate the concept in some halting manner before American independence. He likely did so not from reading Otis, whose pamphlets were not mentioned in his own essays, but rather from reacting against Sir William Blackstone. In his influential *Commentaries on the Laws of England,* published between 1765 and 1769, the only major attempt to codify English law since

Coke's *Institutes* of the previous century, Blackstone explained that sovereignty and Parliament were convertible terms; one could not exist without the other. Indeed, legislature was the greatest act of sovereignty that could be exercised by one being over another. So long as the British constitution lasted, the power of Parliament was absolute and without control. Sovereignty, therefore, was indivisible, unitary, and absolute; hence there could be no check upon the supreme authority of Parliament over America.[9]

To Iredell, this concept—"the great solecism of an *imperium in imperio*"—was "narrow and pedantic," designed "to sacrifice to a point of speculation the happiness of millions"; "if it exists, we are possessed of no liberty; we have nothing we can call our own." It was "the very definition of slavery." The empire, properly examined, was composed "of several distinct and independent legislatures, each engaged within a separate scale, and employed about different objects. The *imperium in imperio* argument is, therefore, not at all applicable to our case, though it has been so vainly and confidently relied on."

Here Iredell was taking a step of great significance beyond the notion of a federal empire, of divided authority, with the colonial legislatures superior in the internal sphere and Parliament superior in the external sphere. Let us repeat that it was for Iredell a reluctant step, one that as Burke said the Americans felt driven to. But could it be defended in legal terms? Iredell felt that it could be in 1774, the same year that James Wilson and Thomas Jefferson penned essays taking a similar position. The heart of their argument was that British authority outside the realm resided solely in the Crown and that during the reign of the first two Stuart kings Parliament had—except for incidental acts—left the colonies alone. Not until the period of Puritan rule in the mid-seventeenth century did the English legislature visibly interpose itself into the picture, a usurpation that continued following the restoration of the monarchy in 1660. The correct relationship between the colonies and the Mother Country was the same as the one that had existed between England and Scotland before the Act of Union in 1707, with each country having its own parliament and joined only through the person of the monarch. If then the colonists were not bound by the edicts of Parliament, why had Americans obeyed the Acts of Trade and Navigation in the years after 1660? They had "assented" to them, explained Iredell, because the laws were just and practical statutes that benefited America as well as England; but in so doing they had bestowed no "Right to indiscriminate Legislation" upon the Lords and Commons.[10]

The colonists had sacrificed none of their fundamental liberties when they settled in the New World. They were the treasure of all citizens of the empire and were anchored in the British constitution. At times, however, Iredell based his stand on both the British constitution and the colonial constitutions, a point of more than passing interest since under our present federal system we live under both state and national constitutions. Although Iredell maintained that Englishmen could not lose their rights under the British constitution by taking up residence in a distant outpost of the empire, those rights were formally reasserted in the colonial charters granted by the king. The "constitution of this country," as Iredell traced it for his own North Carolina, "is founded on the provincial charter, which may well be considered as the original contract between the King and the inhabitants."

Just as Parliament had no suzerainty whatever over the colonies, so it was that there were restraints upon the king's hands. "We respect and reverence the rights of the king," Iredell assured Englishmen; "we owe, and we pay him allegiance, and we will sacredly abide by the terms of our charters. . . . But we will not submit to any alteration of the original terms of the contract." It might be undeniable, admitted Iredell, that a governor's commission from the Crown authorized the colonial executive to endeavor to act in opposition to the wishes of the colonists. "But that the people are bound by a set of rules and instructions" that were "securely locked up in the Governor's strong box" was an absurdity.

At the same time, the Edenton lawyer repeatedly underscored his desire to settle the imperial dispute "on the basis of a general negotiation." The most appropriate body to represent the American view was the Continental Congress, which henceforth should be a permanent intercolonial institution.

He granted that previously there had been no constitutional relationship between the various colonies, that—in a sense— Britons correctly referred to the Congress as an extralegal assemblage. Given the threat to their liberties, however, Americans "justly thought" that "petty constitutional Regards" were "of little consideration." A "Constitution was only valuable as the means of securing *freedom* and *happiness:* When it no longer could serve ... to that end, it was their duty to select other means more *permanent,* and more *effectual.*"

Doubtless Iredell still felt that the London government might appropriately have an important role to play in the areas of war and peace, diplomacy, Indian affairs, and postal matters; but not until such a federal relationship was grafted on to the British constitution by a mutual agreement of England and America. Although Iredell himself never formalized a federal scheme to bring before an imperial conference table, he felt a partial solution to the Anglo-American crisis was contained in the Earl of Chatham's Reconciliation Bill, introduced in the House of Lords on February 1, 1775, since it would "reconcile *substantially,*" if not entirely, "the honest views" on both sides. If the Chatham plan did not renounce the sovereignty of Parliament, it expressly discarded that body's right of American taxation, and it called for the repeal of all laws—except the Quartering Act—passed since 1763 that were opposed by the colonists. Moreover, it provided recognition of the Continental Congress, which would be in charge of external relations with the British government, in addition to overseeing the raising of monies in America for defense. The old Acts of Trade and Navigation were to remain on the books, enforced only under the highly defective machinery of the pre-1763 years. Chatham's blueprint was not entirely to Iredell's liking. Even so, he was willing to be somewhat flexible; and the Chatham bill would at least serve as the basis for an opening dialogue on the subject of defining an enduring constitutional connection between Britain and the American colonies.[11]

In after years when Iredell reflected on the controversies that had exacted the life of an empire, he stated that British statesmanship had failed to "effectually reconcile Power and Liberty" within the family of English-speaking peoples. Since that day Iredell's ideas have had their seasons, not only in Great Britain with the adoption of the notion of Commonwealth relations,[12] but even earlier in America with the triumph of federalism at the conclusion of the Revolutionary era. For notwithstanding the total British rejection of his contention that sovereignty was divisible within the broad, expansive structure of the pre-Revolutionary empire, Iredell continued to believe that the power of political bodies was restrained, that sovereignty—which rested with the people rather than with institutions—might operate in different ways at different political levels.

But whereas in the preindependence years Iredell feared domination by the central government in London at the expense of the local, or colony, governments in America, his concerns after 1776 were in the opposite direction. As a state judge and subsequently as state attorney general of North Carolina, he came to the conclusion that the state legislatures—created by the new state constitutions—behaved at times irresponsibly, acting as though their authority was limitless. They passed unconstitutional laws that in various ways attacked private property and the right of trial by jury at the state level. They also disregarded the legitimate prerogatives of the Congress, which had become a legal body as a result of the ratification in 1781 of the Articles of Confederation, America's first national constitution. Iredell was particularly upset because the state bodies had refused to honor certain provisions of Congress's treaty of peace in 1783 involving treatment of the loyalists and payment of prewar debts to British merchants.

The North Carolina assembly, maintained Samuel Johnston, could not act contrary to fundamental law, to the constitution. But how to constrain the legislature? In 1776 Johnston had himself written that "there can be no check on the Representatives of the People . . . but the people themselves, and in order that the check may be more effectual I would have Annual elections."[13] Johnston's remedy, however had not worked; it was no great improvement over Otis's solution in the 1760s.

As early as 1783—twenty years before John Marshall's

landmark decision in *Marbury v. Madison*—Iredell believed that he had found a cure to the disease of unrestrained legislative action: "in a Republic," he wrote, "the Law is superior to any or all Individuals, and the Constitution superior even to the Legislature, and of which the Judges are the guardians and protectors."[14] Here was as clear and unequivocal an expression of judicial review as perhaps had yet been written in America. Indeed, Iredell detailed the notion even more explicitly four years later as attorney for the plaintiff in the 1787 case of *Bayard v. Singleton,* where he was instrumental in persuading a North Carolina superior court to declare void a law of the state legislature, which, contrary to the state constitution, had eliminated certain types of trial by jury.

In explaining his own reasoning and justifying the court's decision, Iredell drew a direct analogy to the crisis in the old empire. Legislative supremacy in the state of North Carolina was just as repugnant and illegal as Parliamentary supremacy had been previously in the colony of North Carolina. "We had not only been sickened and disgusted for years with the high and almost impious language from Great Britain, of the omnipotent power of the British Parliament, but had severely smarted under its effects." How could one believe that "in the same moment when we spurned at the *insolent despotism* of Great Britain," we would have "established a *despotic* power among ourselves?" Accordingly, he had "no doubt but that the power of the Assembly is limited and defined by the constitution."

When confronted with a choice between "the *fundamental, unrepealable* law," the creation of the people collectively, and a measure at variance with the constitution, "founded on an authority not given by the people, and to which, therefore, the people owed no obedience," the judges' intervention in behalf of the people was "unavoidable." For the constitution was no "mere imaginary thing, about which ten thousand different opinions may be formed, but a written document to which all may have recourse, and to which, therefore, the judges cannot wilfully blind themselves."[15] By appealing to the judiciary to establish the point where lawmaking bodies overstepped their constitutional prerogatives, Iredell was giving expression to an enlarged conception of separation of powers, a doctrine which, as Gordon Wood has observed, was accorded more lip service than actual substance by the drafters of the initial state constitutions.[16] Without judicial review, it is doubtful that separation of powers would ever have been meaningful at any level of American constitutionalism.

But the problem for Iredell and other men of a nationalist orientation in the 1780s involved more than curbing the encroachments of the state legislatures; it likewise called for reinforcing the hand of the national legislature. Once again, Iredell could resort to old arguments, but in a new setting. Just as he had sought in the middle 1770s to demonstrate that England and America could remain equal spokes in the wheel of empire, so he and others tried to show that the sovereignty of the people might be expressed in two ways without threatening the liberties of the people. When all efforts to beef up the power of Congress by means of amendments to the Articles of Confederation failed, Iredell and like-minded leaders took more decisive action.

The federal Constitution of 1787 was the result. Although Iredell did not attend the gathering in Philadelphia that hammered out the new political system, his ideas on institutional reform were well known to Hugh Williamson, William R. Davie, and Richard Dobbs Spaight of the North Carolina delegation; and he in turn was in enthusiastic agreement with their handiwork in the City of Brotherly Love. He energetically joined them in campaigning for the adoption of the Constitution in North Carolina. In January 1788, under the pen name "Marcus," he published his *Answers to Mr. Mason's Objections to the New Constitution*. He demonstrated, among other things, that the legitimate rights of the states would not fall sacrifice to a firmer form of union. As Iredell described the Constitution to the Hillsborough Convention during the ratification contest, "there will be two governments to which we shall owe obedience. To the government of the Union in certain defined cases—to our own state government in every other case."[17] The restructuring of power added additional jurisdiction to the central government without making Congress the final, indivisible and incontestable authority in the nation. The federal and state governments held separate areas of control.

For the first time, Iredell's name became well known outside his state, and that led to greater things. As Hugh Williamson explained from New York, "The North Carolina Debates are considerably read in this place, especially by Congress members; some of whom, who formerly had little knowledge of the citizens of North Carolina, have lately been *very minute in their inquiries concerning Mr. Iredell.*"[18] In February 1790, George Washington appointed Iredell an associate justice of the United States Supreme Court. Only thirty-eight years old, he had nonetheless a wide legal background that stretched over twenty years. And as the president said, Iredell sustained a high "reputation . . . for abilities, legal knowledge, and respectability of character."[19]

As a justice, Iredell demonstrated, in Julius Goebel's words, "a tough and independent outlook." (Clearly the North Carolinian and James Wilson of Pennsylvania possessed the finest legal minds on the high bench in this period.) If Iredell "usually had his own characteristic approach" in seeking a solution to cases before the tribunal, he displayed a firm consistency to principles of the new American federalism. An unwavering nationalist so far as central power over foreign and interstate commerce were concerned (and an ardent supporter of Hamilton's financial program), as in fact he had been since the Revolutionary War, he generally approved positions taken by the Federalist political party in the 1790s. Nevertheless, he showed in such Supreme Court cases as *Chisholm v. Georgia* (1793) and *Ware v. Hylton* (1796) what Goebel describes as "his continuing interest in maintaining watch and ward over the rights of the states."[20]

Yet, consistent with his federalism, he opposed state encroachments on the national government and its officials. For example, he criticized the North Carolina legislature's efforts to instruct and bind the state's United States senators concerning their voting in Congress. Was the honor of the country to "be sullied—its public faith broken—and the Government of the United States to become a mere mockery, merely to gratify the wishes of North Carolina?"[21] Or as he eloquently reminded a Georgia grand jury:

> We ought never forget that there are two Governments to which we owe obedience; each limited, but each perfect in its kind: the State governments, in all instances of authority under their own constitutions, not relinquished to the United States; the Government of the United States, in all instances of authority so relinquished, and of which the Constitution of the United States forms the evidence and the barrier. If this complication of authority requires greater care and attention than formerly, let us remember that we are amply recompensed for it by the greater blessings we enjoy. The happiness of our country certainly depends, not only on the preservation of the State Governments in their due sphere of authority, but on the firm union of the whole for the great purposes of the common welfare of the whole, which fatal experience hath long since told us cannot be secured without an energetic government to effect it.[22]

There is no doubt that Iredell saw judicial review as a legitimate function of the federal courts as well as that of the state courts. There was, to be sure, no precedent for it in the brief history of the Articles of Confederation. In fact, the Confederation government, attempting to use appellate jurisdiction in prize cases, had been rebuffed by the states. Its heritage was a negative one as to both judicial review and national judicial authority. Recent scholarship, however, leaves little if any doubt that the framers at Philadelphia intended its employment by the federal courts; in contrast to the architects of the state constitutions, the Founding Fathers had a deep commitment to the separation of powers. And that carried with it positive implications for judicial review, which quite likely were not expressly stated for fear that opponents of the Constitution would seize upon the issue in the ratifying conventions and defeat it.

Although there was no formal pronouncement or ruling on the subject in the 1790s while Iredell sat on the court, several developments pointed in the direction of federal judicial review. On one occasion, in responding to congressional action calling upon circuit court judges to serve as pension commissioners, Iredell privately informed President Washington that the measure was unconstitutional: it conferred on the judiciary responsibility absent from the Constitution. Whatever else, Iredell saw the federal courts as an active force in the republic, an equal with the other branches of the central government. (In this respect, it may be noteworthy that initially Iredell was the only one of the Supreme Court justices who chose to make his home in the capital city.)

Perhaps there is a lesson for present-day reformers at home and nation-builders abroad in the accomplishments of Iredell's generation. The leaders of the American Revolution were not blinded by their hostility toward the king and his politicians in England to the extent that they wished to destroy all that was their British heritage—they were not haters. The destruction of a colonial-monarchical relationship was about the degree of their negative activity. They were constructive, creative statesmen who shaped institutions which defined the parameters of government and enunciated the liberties of the people. And all this they did in an age of unitary nation-states. Theirs was the first successful federal system of government. Although that system owed much to British antecedents and to American Revolutionary experience—"to the British constitution" and to "proper republican checks," as Iredell put it—relatively few thoughtful men had the vision to see how such a peculiar mixture might be put together and then sustained.[23] James Iredell was one of them.

NOTES

NOTES

2. Did the American Revolution Really Happen?

1. Crane Brinton, *The Anatomy of Revolution* (New York, 1938), pp. 1–21.

2. Ibid.

3. Ibid., passim.

4. For a complete development of this theme, see Robert E. Brown, *Carl Becker on History and the American Revolution* (East Lansing, Mich., 1970), chs. 1 and 4.

5. James Harvey Robinson, *The New History: Essays Illustrating the Modern Historical Outlook* (New York, 1912), chs. 1 and 8; Brown, *Carl Becker*, chs. 1 and 4.

6. Brown, *Carl Becker*, ch. 4.

7. Ibid., chs. 4 and 6.

8. Carl L. Becker, *The History of Political Parties in the Province of New York, 1760–1776*, Bulletin of the University of Wisconsin, History Series, vol. 2 (Madison, 1909), ch. 1.

9. Ibid., chs. 2–10; Brown, *Carl Becker*, ch. 2.

10. Becker, *History of Political Parties*, chs. 10–11; Brown, *Carl Becker*, ch. 3.

11. Becker, *History of Political Parties*, p. 272.

12. Ibid., ch. 11; Brown, *Carl Becker*, ch. 3.

13. Becker, *History of Political Parties*, p. 10, n. 35.

14. Charles A. Beard, *An Economic Interpretation of the Constitution of the United States* (New York, 1913), passim.

15. Ibid., pp. 24–25 and n., 71–72, 246–47, 250–51, et passim.

16. Arthur M. Schlesinger, Sr., *The Colonial Merchants and the American Revolution, 1763–1776* (New York, 1919), passim; idem, *New Viewpoints in American History* (New York, 1922), pp. 47–57, 72–100, 103–9, 160–81, 184–98, 201.

17. J. Franklin Jameson, *The American Revolution Considered as a Social Movement* (Princeton, 1926), passim.

18. Ibid., pp. 18, 27–28, 39–40; Brown, *Carl Becker,* pp. 163–66.

19. Jameson, *American Revolution,* ch. 1.

20. Brinton, *Anatomy of Revolution,* pp. 23–25, 48–49, 58–59, 63, 70, 78, 83, 93, 95, 103, 108–15, 141, 151, 170, 178, 181–82, 205, 209, 216–17, 226.

21. Merrill Jensen, *The Articles of Confederation: An Interpretation of the Social-Constitutional History of the American Revolution, 1774–1781* (Madison, 1940), passim.

22. Robert E. Brown, *Charles Beard and the Constitution: A Critical Analysis of "An Economic Interpretation of the Constitution"* (Princeton, 1956), pp. 4–15.

23. Quoted in Brown, *Carl Becker,* p. 249.

24. Ibid., chs. 8–9.

25. Charles A. Beard and Mary R. Beard, *A Basic History of the United States* (Philadelphia, 1944), passim; and Charles A. Beard, *The Republic: Conversations on Fundamentals* (New York, 1944), passim.

26. For a view of the many writers who were to engage in the dialogue over the Progressive thesis after 1950, see Brown, *Carl Becker,* pp. 261–67. For my own interpretation of colonial society, see Robert E. Brown, *Middle-Class Democracy and the Revolution in Massachusetts, 1681–1780* (Ithaca, N.Y., 1955), chs. 1–6; and Robert E. Brown and B. Katherine Brown, *Virginia, 1705–1786: Democracy or Aristocracy?* (East Lansing, Mich., 1964), passim. The Massachusetts book began as a doctoral dissertation in 1938, before Becker had changed his mind, and was presented at the University of Wisconsin in 1945.

27. Brown, *Middle-Class Democracy,* chs. 7–9.

28. Ibid., chs. 10–14.

29. Ibid., ch. 15; Brown and Brown, *Virginia,* ch. 13.

30. Ibid.; Brown, *Middle-Class Democracy,* ch. 15.

31. Brown, *Charles Beard and the Constitution,* passim.

32. Forrest McDonald, *We the People: The Economic Origins of the Constitution* (Chicago, 1958), passim.

33. Brown, *Carl Becker,* p. 265 and notes.

34. See Jesse Lemisch, "The American Revolution Seen from the Bottom Up," and Staughton Lynd, "Beyond Beard," in *Towards a New Past: Dissenting Essays in American History,* ed. Barton J. Bernstein (New York, 1967), pp. 3–64; Brown, *Carl Becker,* ch. 11.

35. John Adams to H. Niles, Feb. 13, 1818, in John Adams, *The Works of John Adams,* ed. Charles Francis Adams, 10 vols. (Boston, 1850–56), 10:282–83.

36. J. Adams to Dr. J. Morse, Nov. 29, 1815, in John Adams, *The Works of John Adams*, 10:182–83.

37. J. Adams to Abigail Adams, July 3, 1776, in *Familiar Letters of John Adams and His Wife Abigail Adams, During the Revolution,* ed. Charles Francis Adams (Boston, 1875), pp. 191, 193–94.

38. Samuel Adams to Benjamin Kent, July 27, 1776, in Samuel Adams, *The Writings of Samuel Adams,* ed. Harry Alonzo Cushing (New York, 1907), 3:303–5.

39. Alexander Hamilton, *The Papers of Alexander Hamilton,* ed. Harold C. Syrett (New York, 1972), 16:18.

40. Thomas Jefferson, *The Writings of Thomas Jefferson,* ed. Andrew A. Lipscomb (Washington, D.C., 1903), 1:9, 14, 21, 23.

41. Alexis de Tocqueville, *Democracy in America,* ed. Phillips Bradley (New York, 1945), 1:13, 29, 46–47, 54–56, et passim.

3. The Idea of Independence

1. David M. Potter, *The South and the Sectional Conflict* (Baton Rouge, 1968), p. 245.

2. John Adams to Mercy Warren, July 7, 1807, as quoted by Merrill Jensen, "Historians and the Nature of the American Revolution," in *The Reinterpretation of Early American History: Essays in Honor of John Edwin Pomfret,* ed. Ray Allen Billington (San Marino, Calif., 1966), p. 123.

3. Daniel J. Boorstin, *The Genius of American Politics* (Chicago, 1953), pp. 68–69.

4. J. Franklin Jameson, *The American Revolution Considered as a Social Movement* (Boston, [1926], 1956), p. 9.

5. J. M. Bunsted, " 'Things in the Womb of Time': Ideas of American Independence, 1633 to 1763," *William and Mary Quarterly,* 3d ser. 31 (1974): 533–64.

6. Pauline Maier, "Coming to Terms with Samuel Adams," *American Historical Review* 81 (1976), 18–19.

7. This paragraph and the questions following are stated in different form in my introduction to Herbert Friedenwald's *The Declaration of Independence: An Interpretation and an Analysis* (New York, [1904], 1974), pp. xx–xxvii.

8. Carl Becker, "The Spirit of '76," in Carl L. Becker et al., *The Spirit of '76 and Other Essays* (New York, [1927], 1966), p. 55.

9. Samuel Seabury as quoted in Merrill Jensen, *The Founding of a Nation: A History of the American Revolution, 1763–1776* (New York, 1968), pp. 510–11.

10. Charles Lee to Patrick Henry, July 29, 1776, in Charles Lee, *The Lee Papers*, 4 vols. (New York, 1872–75), 2:177.

4. The American Revolution: An Explanation

1. Portions of this essay are adapted from Jack P. Greene, "An Uneasy Connection: An Analysis of the Preconditions of the American Revolution," in *Essays on the American Revolution*, ed. Stephen C. Kurtz and James H. Hutson (Chapel Hill, 1973), pp. 32–80.

2. Thomas Pownall, "The State of the Government of Massachusetts Bay as it stood in ye Year 1757," Colonial Office Papers 325/2 (Public Record Office, London). Italics added.

3. Thomas Barnard, *A Sermon Preached before His Excellency Francis Bernard, Esq., . . . May 25th, 1763* (Boston, 1763), p. 44.

4. [Daniel Leonard], *To the Inhabitants of the Province of Massachusetts Bay*, Feb. 6, 1775, in *The American Colonial Crisis*, ed. Barnard Mason (New York, 1972), p. 56.

5. John Locke, *Two Treatises of Government*, ed. Peter Laslett (Cambridge, Mass., 1960), pp. 462–63.

6. "The Declaration of Independence," July 4, 1776, reprinted in *Colonies to Nation 1763–1789: A Documentary History of the American Revolution*, ed. Jack P. Greene (New York, 1975), pp. 298–301.

7. Edward Shils, "Centre and Periphery," in *The Logic of Personal Knowledge: Essays Presented to Michael Polanyi* (Glencoe, Ill., 1961), pp. 117–24.

8. For an elaboration of these points, see Greene, "An Uneasy Connection," pp. 53–62.

9. See, especially, Bernhard Knollenberg, *Origin of the American Revolution, 1759–1766* (New York, 1960).

10. [Oxenbridge Thacher], *Sentiments of a British American* (Boston, 1764), as quoted by Edwin G. Burrows and Michael Wallace, "The American Revolution: The Ideology and Psychology of National Liberation," *Perspectives in American History* 6 (1972): 191–92.

11. See Richard Koebner, *Empire* (Cambridge, 1961), pp. 105–65.

12. See Lawrence Henry Gipson, "The American Revolution as an Aftermath of the Great War for Empire, 1754–1763," *Political Science Quarterly* 65 (1950): 86–104.

13. Knollenberg, *Origin of the American Revolution*, p. 87.

14. On this point, see Bernard Bailyn, *The Ideological Origins of the American Revolution* (Cambridge, Mass., 1967), pp. 60–85.

15. The impact of the Stamp Act crisis is examined in Edmund S. Morgan and Helen M. Morgan, *The Stamp Act Crisis: Prologue to Revolution* (Chapel Hill, 1953).

16. "Anti-Sejanus" to *London Chronicle,* Nov. 28–30, 1765, in *Prologue to Revolution: Sources and Documents on the Stamp Act Crisis, 1764–1766,* ed. Edmund S. Morgan (Chapel Hill, 1959), p. 100.

17. Quoted by Bernhard Knollenberg, *The Growth of the American Revolution, 1766–1775* (Chapel Hill, 1975), p. 24.

18. "John Plowshare" to *London Chronicle,* Feb. 20, 1766, and "Anti-Sejanus" to *London Chronicle,* Jan. 23, 1766, in *Prologue to Revolution,* ed. Edmund S. Morgan, pp. 103, 131.

19. Lord Northington's statement in the House of Lords, Dec. 17, 1765, as quoted by Knollenberg, *Growth of the American Revolution,* p. 17.

20. *New York Mercury,* Aug. 27, 1764, as quoted by Burrows and Wallace, "The American Revolution," p. 191.

21. Oliver Delancy to Lady Sussannah Warren, Jan. 10, 1766, Peter Warren Papers G/Am/84 (East Sussex Record Office, Lewes, England).

22. See also Merrill Jensen, "The American People and the American Revolution," *Journal of American History* 57 (1970): 5–35.

23. Joseph Reed, *Four Dissertations on the Reciprocal Advantages of a Perpetual Union between Great Britain and her American Colonies* (Philadelphia, 1766), p. 108.

24. John Dickinson to William Pitt, Dec. 21, 1765, Chatham Papers, PRO 30/8/97 (Public Record Office, London).

25. See, for instance, the remarks of William Knox in Jack P. Greene, ed., "William Knox's Explanation for the American Revolution," *William and Mary Quarterly,* 3d ser. 30 (1973): 293–306.

26. See W. Paul Adams, "Republicanism in Political Rhetoric before 1776," *Political Science Quarterly* 85 (1970): 397–421; and Jack P. Greene, "The Preconditions for American Republicanism: A Comment," in Library of Congress, First Symposia on the American Revolution, *The Development of a Revolutionary Mentality: Papers* (Washington, D.C., 1972), pp. 119–24.

27. Charles Inglis, *An American: The True Interest of America Impartially Stated* (Philadelphia, 1776), rpt. in *Revolutionary Versus Loyalist: The First American Civil War 1774–1784,* ed. Leslie F. S. Upton (Waltham, Mass., 1968), p. 76.

28. Ibid., p. 75.

29. See Pauline Maier, *From Resistance to Revolution: Colonial Radicals and the Development of American Opposition to Britain, 1765–1775* (New York, 1972); and Jack P. Greene, "The Alienation of Benjamin Franklin—British American," *Journal of the Royal Society of Arts* 124 (1976), 52–73.

30. The crucially limiting importance of these beliefs is considered

in Jack P. Greene, "The Plunge of Lemmings: A Consideration of Recent Writings on British Politics and the American Revolution," *South Atlantic Quarterly* 67 (1968), 141–75.

31. This is not however to imply that the aims and motives of all opposition elements were the same.

32. In this connection, see Edmund S. Morgan, "The American Revolution Considered as an Intellectual Movement," in *Paths of American Thought,* ed. Arthur M. Schlesinger, Jr., and Morton White (Boston, 1963), pp. 11–33; and Douglass Adair, "Fame and the Founding Fathers," in *Fame and the Founding Fathers: Papers and Comments,* ed. Edmund P. Willis (Bethlehem, Pa., 1967), pp. 27–52.

33. On this process of political mobilization, see R. A. Ryerson, "Political Mobilization and the American Revolution: The Resistance Movement in Philadelphia, 1765–1775," *William and Mary Quarterly,* 3d ser. 31 (1974): 565–88; Pauline Maier, "The Charleston Mob and the Evolution of Popular Politics in Revolutionary South Carolina, 1765–1784," *Perspectives in American History* 4 (1970): 173–96; and Jesse Lemisch, "Jack Tar in the Streets: Merchant Seamen in the Politics of Revolutionary America," *William and Mary Quarterly,* 3d ser. 25 (1968): 371–407.

34. See Richard Maxwell Brown, "Violence and the American Revolution," in *Essays on the American Revolution,* ed. Stephen C. Kurtz and James H. Hutson, pp. 81–120.

35. Richard Champion to Caleb Lloyd, Nov. 1770, in *The American Correspondence of a Bristol Merchant, 1766–1776: Letters of Richard Champion,* ed. G. H. Guttridge (Berkeley, 1934), p. 22.

36. Thomas Jefferson, "A Summary View of the Rights of British America," August 1774, in *Colonies to Nation,* ed. Jack P. Greene p. 231.

37. This theme is developed in Jack P. Greene, "Search for Identity: An Interpretation of the Meaning of Selected Patterns of Social Response in Eighteenth-Century America," *Journal of Social History* 3 (1970): 189–220; Edmund S. Morgan, "The Puritan Ethic and the American Revolution," *William and Mary Quarterly,* 3d ser. 24 (1967): 3–41; and Perry Miller, "From the Covenant to the Revival," in *The Shaping of American Religion* ed. James Ward Smith and A. Leland Jamison (Princeton, 1961), 1: 322–50.

38. Ebenezer Baldwin, "An Appendix Stating the Heavy Grievances the Colonies Labor Under . . . ," Aug. 31, 1774, in *Colonies to Nation,* ed. Jack P. Greene, pp. 213, 217.

39. See David Ammerman, *In the Common Cause: American Response to the Coercive Acts of 1774* (Charlottesville, 1974). The quotation is from North Carolina instructions, Aug. 25, 1774, in "The First Conti-

nental Congress: A Documentary History," ed. Jack P. Greene in U.S. Congress, House, *Commemoration Ceremony in Honor of the Two Hundredth Anniversary of the First Continental Congress,* 93d Cong., 2d Sess., H. Doc. 93–413 (Washington, D.C., 1975), p. 86.

40. Rhode Island Instructions, Aug. 14, 1774, in "The First Continental Congress," ed. Jack P. Greene, p. 80.

41. New Hampshire Instructions, July 21, 1774, in "The First Continental Congress," ed. Jack P. Greene, p. 79.

42. John Adams, Notes on Debates, Sept. 26–27, 1774, in "The First Continental Congress," ed. Jack P. Greene, p. 101.

43. Thomas Falconer to Charles Gray, May 17, 1766, Gray-Round Archives, D/DRg 4/14 (Essex Record Office, Chelmsford, England).

44. See Winthrop D. Jordan, "Familial Politics: Thomas Paine and the Killing of the King, 1776," *Journal of American History* 60 (1973): 294–308; Burrows and Wallace, "The American Revolution," 268–94.

45. Pauline Maier, "The Beginnings of American Republicanism, 1765–1775," in Library of Congress, First Symposia on the American Revolution, *Development of a Revolutionary Mentality: Papers,* pp. 99–117.

46. Dr. Richard Price, "Observations on the Importance of the American Revolution," March 1784, in *Colonies to Nation,* ed. Jack P. Greene, p. 423.

47. The most comprehensive treatment of these loyalists will be found in Robert McCluer Calhoon, *The Loyalists in Revolutionary America, 1760–1781* (New York, 1973), but see also Burrows and Wallace, "The American Revolution," 295–99.

48. Locke, *Two Treatises of Government, pp.* 463—64.

5. John Adams and the Coming of the Revolution

1. General Services Administration, National Archives and Records Service, Office of the Federal Register (OFR), *Public Papers of the Presidents of the United States, John F. Kennedy, . . . 1961* (Washington, D.C., 1962), pp. 634–35.

2. Adams to Warren, Jan. 9, 1787, The Massachusetts Historical Society, *Warren-Adams Letters,* 2 vols. (New York [1917, 1925], 1972), 2: 281.

3. Quoted in L. H. Butterfield, Introduction, in *John Adams: A Biography in His Own Words,* ed. James Bishop Peabody, The Founding Father Series (New York, 1973), p. 6. Subsequent citations are to this one-volume edition.

4. John Adams, *Diary and Autobiography,* ed. L. H. Butterfield, 4

vols., The Adams Papers, Series 1, Diaries (Cambridge, Mass., 1961), 1: 73–78.

5. Butterfield, Introduction, in *John Adams,* ed. James Bishop Peabody, p. 10.

6. Adams, *Diary and Autobiography,* 1:68–69.

7. Edmund S. Morgan, "John Adams and the Puritan Tradition" (Essay Review), *New England Quarterly* 34 (1961): 523.

8. Clinton Rossiter, "The Legacy of John Adams," *Yale Review* 46 (1957): 532.

9. Adams, *Diary and Autobiography,* 1: 82.

10. Ibid., p. 37.

11. Ibid., p. 41.

12. Ibid., pp. 33–34.

13. Ibid., p. 35.

14. Ibid.

15. Ibid., p. 41.

16. Ibid., p. 45.

17. Ibid., p. 57.

18. Ibid., p. 55.

19. Ibid., p. 53.

20. Ibid., p. 43.

21. John Adams, *The Works of John Adams,* ed. Charles Francis Adams, 10 vols. (Boston, 1850–56), 2: 449, 451–52, 462–64.

22. Ibid., pp. 466–67.

23. Adams, *Diary and Autobiography,* 1: 263.

24. Henry S. Commager, ed., *Documents of American History,* 9th ed. (Englewood Cliffs, N.J., 1973), p. 61.

25. *Boston Gazette,* Jan. 13, 20, and 27, 1766.

26. Adams, *Diary and Autobiography,* 3: 287.

27. Ibid.

28. Ibid., 1: 337.

29. Ibid., 3: 306.

30. Ibid.

31. See note 1 in Adams, *Diary and Autobiography,* 1: 339.

32. Ibid., p. 347.

33. Ibid., 3: 289–90.

34. Ibid., pp. 293–94.

35. Ibid., 2: 79.

36. Ibid., 3: 296.

37. Quoted in Samuel Eliot Morison et al., *The Growth of the American Republic,* 6th ed., 2 vols. (New York, 1969), 1: 155.

38. Adams, *Diary and Autobiography,* 2: 7.

39. Ibid., p. 67.

40. Ibid., p. 76.

41. Ibid., p. 77.

42. Alden E. Bradford, ed., *Speeches of the Governors of Massachusettes from 1765 to 1775 and the Answers of the House of Representatives* . . . (Boston, 1818), pp. 336–42, especially p. 340.

43. Ibid., pp. 351–65, especially pp. 363–64. For a brief discussion of the debate between Governor Hutchinson, the Council, and the House of Representatives, see Bernard Bailyn, *The Ordeal of Thomas Hutchinson* (Cambridge, Mass., 1974), pp. 207–10.

44. Adams, *Diary and Autobiography*, 3: 297–98.

45. Quoted in note 1 in Adams, *Diary and Autobiography*, 2: 80.

46. Ibid.

47. Ibid., p. 82.

48. Ibid., p. 86.

49. Ibid., 3: 302.

50. Quoted in Gilbert Chinard, *Honest John Adams* (Boston, 1933), pp. 68–69.

51. Adams, *Diary and Autobiography*, 2: 96.

52. Ibid., pp. 96–97.

53. Ibid., p. 97.

54. John Adams to Abigail Adams, Aug. 28, 1774, in *Familiar Letters of John Adams and His Wife Abigail Adams, During the Revolution*, ed. Charles Francis Adams (Boston, 1875), p. 26.

55. Adams, *Diary and Autobiography*, 2: 120.

56. John Adams to Abigail Adams, Sept. 8, 1774, in *Familiar Letters*, ed. Charles Francis Adams, p. 31.

57. Adams, *Diary and Autobiography*, 3: 309.

58. Ibid., 2: 153.

59. Commager, *Documents of American History*, p. 83.

60. Adams, *Diary and Autobiography*, 2: 140, 152.

61. Worthington Chauncey Ford et al., eds., *Journal of the Continental Congress*, 34 vols. (Washington, D.C., 1904–37), 1: 78.

62. Ibid., p. 102.

63. Adams, *Diary and Autobiography*, 3: 313.

64. Ibid., p. 314.

65. John Adams, *The Works of John Adams*, 4: 13, 17, 52.

66. Adams, *Diary and Autobiography*, 3: 315.

67. See John Adams to Abigail Adams, June 17, 1775, in *Familiar Letters*, ed. Charles Francis Adams, pp. 65–66.

68. Commager, *Documents of American History*, p. 95.

69. See note 1, Adams, *Diary and Autobiography*, 2: 162.

70. Ibid., 3: 321.

71. Adams to Warren, July 24, 1775, in Massachusetts Historical Society, *Warren-Adams Letters*, 1: 88.

72. See note 1, Adams, *Diary and Autobiography*, 2: 175.

73. Adams to Horatio Gates, Mar. 23, 1776, see note 6 in *Adams Family Correspondence*, 4 vols., ed. L. H. Butterfield, The Adams Papers, Series 2, Adams Family Correspondence (Cambridge, Mass., 1963), 1: 401.

74. John Adams to Abigail Adams, Mar. 19, 1776, in Adams, ed., *Familiar Letters*, p. 146.

75. John Adams, *The Works of John Adams*, 4: 193, 198, 200.

76. Adams, *Diary and Autobiography*, 3: 383.

77. John Adams to Abigail Adams, May 17, 1776, in John Adams, *Letters of John Adams, Addressed to His Wife*, ed. Charles Francis Adams (Boston, 1841), 1: 109.

78. Quoted in *John Adams*, ed. James Bishop Peabody, p. 197.

79. Commager, *Documents of American History*, p. 100.

80. John Adams to Timothy Pickering, Aug. 6, 1822, in *John Adams*, ed. James Bishop Peabody, p. 201.

81. Stockton and Jefferson quoted by John H. Hazelton, *The Declaration of Independence: Its History* (New York, 1906), p. 162.

82. Lester J. Cappon, ed., *The Adams-Jefferson Letters: The Complete Correspondence between Thomas Jefferson and Abigail and John Adams*, 2 vols. (Chapel Hill, N.C., 1959).

83. Page Smith, *John Adams*, 2 vols. (Garden City, N.Y., 1962).

84. John Adams, *John Adams: A Biography in His Own Words*, ed. James Bishop Peabody, The Founding Father Series, 2 vols. (New York, 1973). Also published in a one-volume edition.

85. In addition to the *Diary and Autobiography* and the *Adams Family Correspondence* cited above, the following works pertaining to John Adams are now in print: *The Earliest Diary of John Adams* (Cambridge, Mass., 1966); *The Legal Papers of John Adams*, 3 vols. (Cambridge, Mass., 1963); and *Portraits of John and Abigail Adams* (Cambridge, Mass., 1967). Among other publications in The Adams Papers are the *Diary of Charles Francis Adams*, 6 vols. (Cambridge, Mass., 1964–74); and *Portraits of John Quincy Adams and His Wife* (Cambridge, Mass., 1970).

86. Butterfield, Introduction, in *John Adams*, ed. James Bishop Peabody, p. 11.

87. 68 (1963), 478–80.

88. OFR, *Public Papers of the Presidents*, p. 637.

6. James Iredell and the Origins of American Federalism

1. Mason L. Weems, *The Life of Washington,* ed. Marcus Cunliffe (Cambridge: Mass. [1800], 1962), p. 168.

2. Clyde Wilson, "Griffith John McRee: An Unromantic Historian of the Old South," *North Carolina Historical Review* 47 (1970): 1–23. See Griffith J. McRee, *The Life and Correspondence of James Iredell,* 2 vols. (New York, 1857–58). I am currently preparing an edition of Iredell's writings, of which the first two volumes have recently appeared: *The Papers of James Iredell* (Raleigh, N.C., 1976).

3. Johnston's voluminous papers are at Hayes Plantation near Edenton, N.C. Microfilm copies are in the Southern Historical Collection, University of North Carolina at Chapel Hill.

4. Quotations from these essays, which form the basis for much of the early portion of this study, will not be footnoted each time they appear. For I have taken material from all in such a way as to weave together Iredell's views on imperial federalism. They are as follows: "Essay on the Court Law Controversy," Sept. 10, 1773; "To the Inhabitants of Great Britain," Sept. 1774; "The Principles of an American Whig," [1775–76?]; [Causes of the American Revolution], June 1776, all in *Papers of James Iredell,* ed. Don Higginbotham, 1: 163–65, 251–68, 328–38, 370–412.

5. My thinking on federalism is derived in considerable measure from Andrew C. McLaughlin's stimulating essay, "The Background of American Federalism," *American Political Science Review* 12 (1918): 213–24.

6. Elliott Barkan, ed., *Edmund Burke on the American Revolution: Selected Speeches and Letters* (New York, 1966), pp. 85. 86.

7. The best treatment of this subject is still Charles F. Mullett, *Fundamental Law and the American Revolution* (New York, 1933).

8. For an analysis of Otis's position, see Bernard Bailyn, *The Ideological Origins of the American Revolution* (Cambridge, Mass., 1967), pp. 176–80. Otis's *Rights of the British Colonies* is in *Pamphlets of the American Revolution,* ed. Bernard Bailyn (Cambridge, Mass., 1965), 1: 409–82.

9. Sir William Blackstone, *Commentaries on the Laws of England,* 4 vols. (London, 1765–69), Book 1, sec. 4, especially pp. 105–8.

10. C. H. McIlwain, in *The American Revolution: A Constitutional Interpretation* (New York, 1924), sides with the Iredell view. In disagreement is R. L. Schuyler, *Parliament and the British Empire* (New York, 1929). Another look at the question, somewhat sympathetic to McIlwain, is Harvey Wheeler, "Calvin's Case (1608) and the

McIlwain-Schuyler Debate," *American Historical Review* 61 (1956): 587–97.

11. William Cobbett, ed., *Parliamentary History of England . . .* , 36 vols. (London, 1806–20), 18: 198–203; James Iredell to Joseph Hewes, June 28, 1775, in *Papers of James Iredell,* ed. Don Higginbotham, 1: 309.

12. An excellent account of how American writers such as Iredell anticipated the British Commonwealth in their thinking is in Randolph G. Adams, *Political Ideas of the American Revolution,* 3d ed. (New York, 1958), pp. 187–88.

13. Samuel Johnston to [?], July 11, 1784, Hayes Papers, Southern Historical Collection, University of North Carolina at Chapel Hill; Johnston to Iredell, Apr. 20, 1776, in *Papers of James Iredell,* ed. Don Higginbotham, 1: 350–51.

14. "Resolutions of the Citizens of Edenton," Aug. 1, 1783; "Instructions to Chowan Representatives," Sept. [?], 1783, Charles E. Johnston Papers, North Carolina Division of Archives and History, Raleigh, North Carolina.

15. McRee, *Iredell,* 2: 145–49, 169–70, 172–76.

16. Gordon Wood, *The Creation of the American Republic* (Chapel Hill, N.C., 1969), pp. 150–61.

17. James Iredell, *Answers to Mr. Mason's Objections to the New Constitution,* in *Pamphlets on the Constitution of the United States,* ed. Paul L. Ford (Brooklyn, 1888), pp. 333–70; Jonathan Elliot, ed., *The Debates in the Several State Conventions on the Adoption of the Federal Constitution . . .* , (Philadelphia, 1891), 4: 35.

18. Hugh Williamson to Iredell, Aug. 12, 1789, McRee, *Iredell,* 2: 265.

19. John C. Fitzpatrick, ed., *The Diaries of George Washington* (Boston, 1925), 4: 85–86.

20. Julius Goebel, Jr., *History of the Supreme Court: Antecedents and Beginnings to 1801* (New York, 1971), pp. 753, 783.

21. Iredell to John Hay, Apr. 19, 1791, Johnson Papers, North Carolina Division of Archives and History.

22. McRee, *Iredell,* 2: 348.

23. Iredell, *Answers to Mr. Mason's Objections to the New Constitution,* in *Pamphlets on the Constitution,* ed. Paul L. Ford, p. 351.

INDEX

INDEX